Managing
MIL

You and your Mother-in-Law
– for better, or for worse?

Katy Rink

Peridot Press

First Published 2013

by Peridot Press

12 Deben Mill Business Centre, Old Maltings Approach,
Melton, Woodbridge, Suffolk IP12 1BL

Tel: 01394 389850 Fax: 01394 386893
Email: enquiries@peridot.co.uk
Website: www.peridot.co.uk

ISBN: 978 1 909 717 00 8

Set and designed by Theoria Design

Contents

MEET THE MILs

Note from the author

I hope that whether you are a bride-to-be, an experienced daughter-in-law, or perhaps a mother-in-law looking for some insight, you will enjoy reading in these pages how other women manage this infamously tricky relationship and draw strength from knowing you are not the only one.

I am indebted to all of the ladies of Shrewsbury who agreed to be interviewed, under a cloak of secrecy, for this book. Without their stories I would have been forced to find material under my own roof and that would have got me into terrible trouble.

Their comments have brought this book to life. Thank you all – you know who you are. Also, to my mother-in-law for being brave enough and big-hearted enough to allow me to do this, in the first place. I hope I haven't let her down.

If MILs and DILs everywhere could take a step back on reading this and think about where they might be able to improve things, then I will have done my 'job'. Where do tensions arise? Why do we react in certain ways? What are the alternatives? I would hope the reader might conclude that with more effort, it is possible to get back on track and become closer as a family.

Writing this has certainly caused me to look closely at my own behaviours and I hope to become a better daughter-in-law for it. Yes, really.

Read it in whatever order you will; dip in and out, pluck out the funny bits or turn to the more serious pieces and see how your own experiences match up. Enjoy it, be entertained but, above all, be inspired to do better.

Introduction

Mothers-in-law have been sorely abused by comics through the ages; traditionally, it has always been the wife's mother who is characterised as an interfering, hen-pecking nuisance. Perhaps it is high time for a change?

This book is not a retaliatory dig at *his* mother. There are stories that will make your toes curl and anecdotes to entertain and amuse but I hope that for the most part, I have allowed myself to be guided by goodwill and a genuine desire to promote family unity.

***

A friend of mine once found her old school picture hidden at the bottom of a drawer in the guest bedroom, following her mother-in-law's visit. Her face had been scratched out with a biro. She thought about confronting MIL about it but wisely let it be. Some things are better left to rest.

Her poor mother-in-law must have been suffering greatly to have taken such dramatic action. But however much she might have desired it in that moment of madness, daughter-in-laws cannot be scratched out, no more than can mothers-in-law. From the moment we say "I do", or sign up to live together in any other meaningful fashion, husband, wife and mother-in-law are committed to each other forever in a kind of awkward *ménage à trois* that none of us have solicited but that all of us have to manage as best as we can, for the rest of time, or at least until MIL snuffs it, or loses her marbles.

The MIL-DIL relationship is like no other we have ever experienced. We start off, tentatively, with no expectations and certainly no real idea of how significant this relationship will become. We behave respectfully, at a distance at first but, sooner or later, our universes will collide and we will have to learn to moderate our behaviour to accommodate MIL and the 'other' family.

It is a steep learning curve and there are many forces at work, conspiring to derail the relationship, but with proper nurturing and understanding, unwanted though it may be in the first instance, it can succeed and mothers and daughters-in-law can remain on good terms and even grow to love one another.

I have blundered through the years managing my own mother-in-law (and vice-versa), making mistakes, learning from them and making them again. She is a big character and potentially a fearsome opponent (you would want her on your side) but we survive in a climate of goodwill and mutual respect and over time, real love. It still frightens me how quickly all the good feeling can curdle and sour the milk of human kindness – over certain flashpoint issues – yet, I suspect, this is the biological imperative taking over. We are programmed to react in certain ways to particular stimuli. Throw in a bit of bad chemistry (those pesky hormones) and you have a perfect storm.

We are very different people but we have learned to identify common ground and to profit from it. We iron out the bumps, gloss over our differences and take delight in our shared primary interest – my two naughty, little boys.

I have at times flailed around in despair, gnashing my teeth and barking at the moon over her behaviour, as I am sure she has at mine. The relationship is a fascinating, tumultuous dynamic that demands constant attention. I write this book in great fear of upsetting her. I accept full responsibility for my part in any of the 'blips' in our history to date and I draw from those experiences here only in so far as they may be of use to other DILs and MILs struggling to stay on course.

I by no means claim to be an expert on MILs in general. I speak with no authority other than having maintained a functional (if fluctuating) rapport with my own mother-in-law for more than a decade.

Each and every relationship will have its own peculiar quirks and sticking points, depending on the personalities involved. I do believe, however, that there are certain truths common to all MIL-DIL pairings and it is those that I seek to examine in writing this book. So here goes…

Rule number one

There is one rule that underpins all other advice offered in this book; it is the single most essential tool in the art of mother-in-law management. If you remember nothing else from this book, remember this:

Try to see things her way ... or at least act as though you do!

For a start, you should know that there is an unspoken truth that colours everything: you're sleeping with her son. A cheap observation, but there it is. YOU'RE SLEEPING WITH HER SON, as in physically intimate, flesh on flesh. She can't get it out of her head. She sees you at it in her sleep. She imagines she can hear it going on when you are under her roof. Every bed creak, every groan of the old bricks and mortar and you are there in megapixels, humping *her* son.

This goes right to the core. You are the cold steel lodged in her heart. The tiniest tweak and she is convulsed with pain. She is absolutely at your mercy and very likely, you don't even know it.

A mother's love for her son should never be underestimated. My seven-year old likes to bury his head in my chest. He is an excellent fit and I press my face into the crook of his neck and breathe him in. If I could dislocate my jaw and gobble-him up, I just might. I made him, so I get to eat him.

The biological threads binding mother and son are a *physical* reality. And you my dear DIL, you wade in and hack right through them, chopping away with your pretty little ways and beguiling charm; a scythe behind your back and not an ounce of regret. There is not the slightest bit of recognition for the twenty, or thirty-odd years of devotion that your poor MIL has heaped upon that form. Not from you or your new husband. That's the bit that really stings. He dives in, drinking you up without so much as a glance backwards.

And so to the crux of the problem: *men*. Most of them are dreadful communicators; they leave all that to us women, whether we like it or not. They lack the emotional intelligence to maintain a successful familial relationship unaided by feminine skill.

It is the husband who gives his mother the chop, not the new bride. But be under no illusions that MIL will ever see it that way. She will not think badly of him, no matter how callously he severs that bond. No matter how many times he forgets to send a Mother's Day card or remember her birthday. She cannot. The truth is too painful; she has to turn on you.

This blame is your burden and you will carry it forever, through all the years of married life. If you work really, really hard you can soften it, lighten it, and conspire between you and your MIL to pretend it's not there. But do not imagine that you will ever cast it off completely. Do not proceed with such foolish confidence, for that would be to underestimate the powers of nature at work here, the inescapable biological forces that are bigger than the both of you.

DIL Club

"I'll have to ring my husband first and make sure he doesn't mind."

"Don't tell him I'm here!"

"Shush, can't talk now – he's listening – but I've got a few crackers I'll tell you in private."

"You're sure you're changing all the names? I'm dead meat, otherwise."

An underground society of daughters-in-law – come to be known as 'DIL Club' – has been key to unlocking the secrets of the MIL-DIL relationship.

There were whispers throughout town for months. Mums at the school gate could talk about nothing else. Have you been? Who was there? What did they say?

DILs would arrive at secret locations of an evening, in groups of five or six at a time, sit down, open a bottle of wine and begin to vent; not all of it was negative, I hasten to add. This wasn't 'stitch and bitch' without the knitting. It was an opportunity for all sorts of different women to share stories – good and bad – about their mothers-in-law. They needed little encouragement!

Everything written here has been shaped by observations gathered during these evenings. There are horror stories, but there are also insights from smart women who have spent time, effort and mental energy managing their own relationships. Tuning in to this powerful, collective wisdom has certainly helped me view things more objectively.

Weighing our grievances against experiences of others helps us keep things in perspective. There are valuable insights and tips, which I hope may be of use to new or struggling DILs and allow them to establish and maintain (at the very least) functional relationships with mothers-in-law.

I would like think that you may be inspired to host your own DIL Clubs, from time to time. You could borrow your book club for a night – why not take time out of *War and Peace*? (a variation on a theme!) Or take along this book to spark a general discussion?

Talking things through with friends who understand helps us stay balanced and remain objective; airing things in an environment where we feel safe and valued, respected and listened to, may be just what we need. Besides, it is great fun and a wonderful ice-breaker for women who don't know one-another very well.

DIL Club is really a support group. Women who are at breaking point struggling to contain an impossible MIL may find great comfort in talking to others in the same boat. Normalising the situation helps relieve the emotional charge. Far better to talk to other women than to a husband who is unfailingly confused by 'feelings', conflicted in his loyalties and in reality, more likely to side with his mother who raised him for thirty-odd years.

I have found that small groups work better, of around five or six friends, otherwise people tend to talk amongst themselves and the shared wisdom is lost.

Why not have a bash at making the all-new 'Mother-in-Law' cocktail to get the conversation rolling? (see recipe on page 207). A good way into the subject is to ask people for their top ten tips for managing MIL. That is usually all it takes to prompt several hours of lively discussion and guaranteed hilarity.

There is only one, simple rule, borrowed from the film *Fight Club*. **You do not talk about DIL Club.**

Unless, of course, one were to write a book about it.

So, let's lift the lid on DIL Club. In the interests of world peace (at least in this part of Shrewsbury), all names have been changed…

She said what?!

Sometimes, dear MILs will come out with things that can turn the milk sour; quips that smart and leave us reeling. It takes us a good few minutes to pick our jaws back off the floor. I am interested to know – do they plan these in advance? Are they premeditated? Do they sleep with a pencil and notepad by the bed in case inspiration comes in their sleep? Do they share them around, cackling with their friends? I mean, are there websites for this stuff?

Here are a few of the choicest comments to have escaped MILs' lips to date. Are we DILs being over-sensitive here? You decide!

66 We were talking about going out for Sunday lunch, discussing some nice places. She chimed in with: 'why don't you go and get married whilst you're at it, then my grandson won't be a bastard.'"

"My MIL is a nasty old biddy. When Dan told her we were getting married, I hid behind the door to see what she would say. When she told him she thought it most likely that I was after his money, I leapt out and said: 'Ooh! There's money? No-one told me.'"

"I was with MIL one day dropping my son off at nursery and he was going through a very clingy stage, so we had a bit of a nightmare leaving him there. As we were going out the door, MIL turns to the child-minders and said: 'I think it's the mother who has separation anxiety, here.' I wanted to punch her lights out."

"She was with my kids watching these walruses lounging on crowded beaches in *The Blue Planet*. I was making tea in the kitchen next door but I could still hear them. She says to my two: 'Look at that big fat walrus, he's got blubber just like mummy's'. I just stood there, holding my wooden spoon with my mouth open.'"

"I remember telling MIL that my husband and I had decided, once and for all, that we wouldn't be having any more babies. Without hesitating, she chimed in: 'Well, of course you'll have your tubes tied'. I was completely stunned. All the dads I know have had vasectomies. It was as though she couldn't bear the idea of her boy having his bits chopped off. Or perhaps she was keeping her fingers crossed for a second crop of grandchildren with a more suitable wife."

"When we found out I was pregnant for the fourth time, we were on our way back from our scan when we phoned MIL to break the good news. She was on loudspeaker in the car, but she didn't realise. As soon as Martin told her, she went absolutely quiet. Then she came out with: 'I can't believe you didn't have her sterilised'. I couldn't believe what I had just heard. I thought she was talking about a cow for a minute. I mouthed at Martin to put the phone down, as she didn't realise I could hear but she went on to say: 'When I had my second, I got myself sterilised straight away. Private education is so important – how on earth are you going to afford it now?'
She was worried about the size of our house and whether we'd need a new car. Usually, Martin never stands up to his parents, but this time, he said: 'Look mother, we're planning on having quite a few more, so we'll be getting a minibus and we'll put a caravan in the back garden.'
After that day, I haven't been able to have quite the same relationship with her. I can't be all gushing now I've seen her in that light."

"When we moved into our first house together, I remember very clearly MIL coming to visit. She walked right in to the hallway, dumped her case and ran her finger across the top of one of our pictures, announcing: 'housekeeping, Sarah!' I thought she was joking for a minute, until I saw the dust."

"I used to work for a nightclub. When I told MIL she said: 'Oh, so you're a hostess?' I asked my husband what she meant – was I just some pay as you go, cheap tart? He said 'oh, she didn't mean that', but I'm a woman. I know she did. She's very clever like that."

"My husband works in the hospital and often flies out of the door at 7.30am, before the children and I have got downstairs. He gets his lunch in the hospital canteen. My MIL clearly thinks it a scandal that I'm not making him a packed lunch every day. She once told me: 'Well, if you won't make his sandwiches there are plenty of pretty nurses who will'."

"When my husband and I moved into our house we were so excited. We invited the in-laws to come and see it. MIL is a terrible snob. It wasn't at all what she would have wanted for their son – I think she thought he should have married some landed Duchess – we are in the middle of town in a semi-detached house. MIL walked into the hallway and looked around her in silence. Then she turned to her husband and said: 'Oh, Geoffrey, didn't we once know some people who lived in a house like this. You remember, what were their names again?' She was quiet all afternoon and then, when we were in the local park with the kids, a cyclist went past her and hawked a load of snot from his nose, spitting it in her direction. It almost landed on her foot and she couldn't take it. She said: 'I really don't like this area. It's not an area I would have expected Simon to live in.' After that day, they've only ever come for a cup of tea."

"I was having Sunday lunch at the in-laws, with all my husbands' brothers and their families around the table as well as my father-in-law. The conversation turned to breast-feeding; MIL is a La Leche counsellor and was very interested to know how things were going. I was a bit uncomfortable discussing it in front of everyone, to start with and then, in the middle of serving the crumble, she comes out with: 'Have you ever had thrush Kathryn?' I wanted the floor to open up underneath me. The boys were peeing themselves laughing. I think I said something like: 'I can't believe you just asked me that'."

"I had been studying for a degree and had put on quite a bit of weight. I happened to mention to my MIL that I was thinking of going on a diet. She said: 'Oh, my dear, you are of an age when you won't ever lose your weight'."

"My fiancé told his mum that he had proposed – she spun round to me and said: 'don't worry, we'll whip you into shape.'"

"We were all at the Christmas dinner table together, fairly early on in our relationship, when MIL started recounting this story about finding my husband in bed with another girl. Everyone else at the table knew the story and knew who she was except me. I couldn't believe what I was hearing.

"I was getting on a bit in age and we hadn't had kids yet, when I told MIL I would be changing jobs. She came out with: 'don't you know it will be another two years before you are eligible for maternity leave?'"

"When it was obvious we were getting serious, MIL let herself into our flat and taped an article about pre-nups to our fridge and said, casually: 'I've left you both a little something on the fridge door'."

"She once said, of my son: 'He's such a bright spark and has such a great sense of humour – he's definitely his father's son.' I'm not sure she realised how that might sound but it didn't give me a great deal of credit! "

"MIL often says of my husband that he's missing 'home' – meaning her home."

"She told me that she just adores her puppies – that they are the replacement for the grandchildren she never sees. **99**

Why is it so all so tricky?

The most commonly given explanation for relationship difficulties between mother-in-law and daughter-in-law is that they are competing for the husband's affection.

This is not my experience; whenever MIL is staying, my husband takes the opportunity for a little down time, absenting himself from family duties. MIL and I are not competing for morsels of appreciation and attention; we forget he is even in the house.

Perhaps the competition is more subtle than that (on DIL's side, at least), aligned with a desire to prove herself a capable wife and mother; the anxiety of being found wanting when held up against MIL's example. It is a struggle for household dominance.

"You know who makes the best apple pie/lemon meringue/ marmalade/beef wellington…," my husband will chuckle, whenever I put his dinner in front of him.

Yes, I know. Your mum. I could kill him, especially as we both know it is true.

I'm going to get it in the neck for this, but I would venture that this is very much a female problem. We are emotional creatures, so much more tuned-in than our men. That has obvious advantages – we are better communicators, peacemakers and social engineers – but it also makes for a lot of unnecessary nail-biting. We waste a lot of mental energy on spurious or imaginary problems, often of our own making. Also, we tend to be more defensive and territorial, suspicious of others' intent – like lionesses protecting our territory. Perhaps we all need to pretend to be blokes for a bit and occupy that brain space with something more fun:

Imagine our men at 'SIL Club'. They'd all be sitting round with tins of beer in awkward silence, until someone coughs and says: "So, how's your father-in-law then?".

The other bloke shrugs: "He's all right ... did you see the game last night?"

Perhaps investing too much thought in it sends the relationship askew. At least we care.

I cannot speak for MILs. I can only imagine how uncomfortable it must be to hand over a beloved son to a girl you barely know.

MIL thinks to herself: "This woman cannot know his value. She will never be able to give him what he deserves. Anything she does will fall short. Must I stand and watch him go to ruin; my high hopes for his brilliant future dashed on her benighted, un-swept doorstep?"

This is all very overblown, of course. Many MILs are delighted that their sons have found happiness with another soul – and a happiness that may lead to grandchildren. Or, at least, that is what MIL will tell DIL, and her friends, and herself (repeatedly), in order to stave off those baser, negative sentiments.

So why can't we all just get along? Is it because:

- she can't let go of her son (forget apron strings, try umbilical cord!)

- you are in competition

- you are doing her job

- you are primed to take everything as a criticism

- you are ungrateful

- you won't listen to her advice

- she doesn't appreciate that you are a grown-up

- she is afraid that you will cut her out

- you prioritise your own mother over her

The daughters-in-law were not backward in coming forwards on this one:

66 It's a woman's inner instinct to want to look after men. It's something primeval. He is her little boy. She needs to see that you are doing it properly."

"As soon as I announced I was pregnant my MIL said, 'I hope it's a boy because that will be like getting my son back'."

"The MIL has a tendency to cling to her son, in a way she doesn't with daughters. She is very protective of him – she knows the daughter can well look after herself, but that a son will need caring for."

"DIL is looking after MIL's son. MIL has previous entitlement. Case closed. She's like a tyrant trying to hold on to his power once she's been ousted."

"I think what they really want is my husband back, the way he was before he married. No-one will ever be good enough for him."

"MIL feels she has grown this child inside her, for another person to wreck his life. She wants him to carry on being a child for a bit longer. She panics that she wasn't done yet – she didn't instil in him everything she'd have liked to."

"I think it's more of a territorial thing. It can be tricky when MIL treats DIL's house as her own. She goes in, sits down, helps herself to a cup of tea, whatever, thinking 'this is my son's house, I can do what I like'."

"When it's your own mum you are unguarded - if she does something annoying you can just tell her but with MIL you can't. You're both always worried about doing and saying the right thing and you sort of tiptoe round one another, awkwardly."

"You've got your own mum. What do you need his mother for? She doesn't really have a place anymore."

"It's about learning to have mutual respect with someone with whom you would probably never choose to become friends with. You have to take the time to learn how to get along."

"You as daughter-in-law will never be truly 'family'. You are not blood, no matter how much you do for them."

"She is simultaneously a visitor – where strict protocol applies – and a member of the family, where she might think she can cross normal barriers. No-one quite knows how to behave."

"If you are someone who has quite a fragile sense of self and this woman comes into your life, all guns blazing, you might feel sensitive and prickly. I think the more comfortable you are with yourself, the easier it might be to get on with your MIL."

"The difficulties arise where the wife allows the MIL too much influence, usually because she cares too much about her good opinion. My MIL was always so bossy. She was the same with my husband but he didn't notice. If he didn't want to do something, he wouldn't do it. With me, I cared too much what she thought. She used to come in and dump on me and I'd nearly break myself over it."

"They come in and treat you like a child and then you always feel you have to justify yourself. She'll say things like 'don't think I'm interfering, but…' and your hackles go up immediately. It's textbook stuff."

"They have a tendency to treat the wives as second-class citizens."

"They simply make judgments about what they see, without stepping back and recognising that you are on a continuous journey."

"It's never simple between women. We are moody and changeable and sometimes, we just meet at the wrong time. Men will have an argument and be able to let it go and never look back, but women don't seem to be able to do that. We're quite petty and we don't forget. It will always be there in the background of the relationship."

"It's also about what baggage you carry with you going into the relationship. If you have had a messed-up childhood and a difficult relationship with your own mother then you might have a harder time with your mother-in-law. If you grew up in a warm, loving and open family where it was okay to be yourself and where a person has room to grow, you might be more appreciative when MIL comes in and just wants to help. If you felt under pressure and judged at home, you may find it difficult to accept that help and see it as some kind of judgment or criticism."

"DILs might be accused of 'changing' the husband, when really he has only moved on. It's that old thing people say: 'my son's my son till he gets a wife…'."

"I think if there is a simple personality clash there to start with, her being your mother-in law blows it out of all proportion."

"My husband put it quite neatly – he said 'there just isn't room in this family for two strong women'."

"I was divorced, Polish and I'd had a baby out of wedlock. Now I look back and I think, how can it have taken me so long for me to figure out why she didn't like me?! To them, these were insurmountable obstacles."

"In my case, things got off to a very bad start on my wedding day, thanks to my father, who told MIL: 'Well, you know this marriage won't last. She's too lazy.' Comparing my father with MIL would be like putting together a snake and a bit of tissue paper – they inhabited different universes. She would have taken his comment absolutely at face value. She thought if a *man* would say that about his *own* daughter, on her wedding day, then she must be the most selfish and lazy woman alive. What a wicked thing to say to a simple and honest woman. He was a wicked truth-sayer. She obviously thought the first thing she had to do was to teach me to dust and mop. She never had a job like me. Temperamentally, we were absolute opposites."

"My world is a world she just doesn't understand. We are singing from different hymn sheets.

99

A little decorum goes a long way

(And a lesson from Carolyn Bourne...)

Something as simple as a greeting can strike fear into the heart of a fledgling daughter-in-law.

I remember dreading arrivals and departures of the in-laws in the early days, due to a lack of social grace on my part and an inability to carry off the French *faire la bise*-style greetings without breaking into a sweat and spraining an ankle. I would hang back, until someone came at me and then panic after one kiss, hoping we'd stop there, pause too long and then clash somewhere in the middle, apologising like mad.

The rotten truth of it, I fear, is that state school education pretty much guarantees social anxiety of this kind. My public school peers dance along a line of farewells in an ecstasy of 'mwah-ing', as if all the underlying tensions of relationships have miraculously evaporated for that one, decorous moment. My brain is screaming "This is awful. You know I hate it, I know you do. Let's quit pretending, and run."

My number one tip here is to launch in first. Take the lead and make it very clear you're going for a double kiss, or hit it hard on one cheek and then take a very deliberate step backwards. It gets it over with and if they fail to follow your lead, it is their screw-up, not yours.

My second tip is to remember that no-one will cling to the memory of an awkward hello. Sure, it might feed into an overall impression of you as being a little gauche or unpolished but they might think far worse of you than that.

My final tip is that you won't be the only one feeling uncomfortable; chances are, you all will – until you get to know one another better, that is.

I now realise that my father-in-law dreads these moments even more than I do. He flinches on approach. I can only imagine the terror he feels as I bear down on him, all bosom and bingo wings.

I have determined to banish awkwardness with enthusiasm and clench him all the more tightly for it. I am very fond of my father-in-law and hope that good feeling will in some way make up for acute physical discomfort on these occasions.

All DILs might pick up a few good manners from the now infamous mother-in-law Carolyn Bourne, who you may have read about in the news a couple of years ago. Following an uncomfortable visit from her daughter-in-law to be, Mrs Bourne sent the poor girl an email in which she lambasted her for her 'staggering uncouthness and lack of grace'. The email went viral and reached millions of readers, via the national press. The future MIL identified poor table manners and a failure to send a thank-you card as specific failings. She even suggested future DIL might consider a finishing school, in order to gain acceptance by 'the wider Bourne family'.

Her email is born of the culture clash between outmoded standards of deportment and the behavioural mores of the mainstream, where an email thank-you, or even a quickfire text, will do. Heaven forbid that we younger generation should sit on our hands whilst our own food goes cold, waiting for the last guest to be served. We pride ourselves on being unfettered by such tedious conventions.

MIL, however, sees it as a failure of personal morality, typifying the selfish society that she imagines is gnawing at the fabric of civilisation.

Perhaps Mrs Bourne did us all a favour, in spelling out what the more decorous, 'traditional' MILs might really be thinking when we lean over great-grandpa to grab a second helping of trifle.

If you have this sort of MIL (identifiable by her vintage pearl earrings and cashmere cardigan) then it would be wise to tune in and pay lip-service to convention, not because you accept the protocol but out of simple respect for her feelings.

If etiquette has not been drummed into you from an early age, chances are you will have a few gaps. Here are some top tips for surviving a weekend with the in-laws:

- Arrive with flowers (from your garden, prettily arranged), a homemade gift (green tomato chutney, made with the last of the summer crop) or at the very least, a bottle of wine.

- Bring your own towel and shampoo.

- Do warn her if you are going to be late as she may be cooking. Don't change plans at the last minute as she will have shopped and planned for the weekend – even if your partner says she won't mind. She will and *you* will get the blame (men will always get away with this but *you*, apparently, should know better).

- Don't nip off to meet friends or, if you have children, expect her to babysit without clearing it with her first.

- Don't let your children rampage through her house (feet most definitely OFF the sofa).

- Do accept offer of pre-dinner drink; it will make you less nervy at the table.

- Don't drink her cellar dry; she might think you have a problem and besides, *in vino veritas* can get you into trouble.

- Do mind your table manners (look them up in a book – not this one, sorry).

- Never head up to bed without wishing MIL goodnight/thanking her for a lovely dinner.

- If you wake up first, offer to make tea/coffee for everyone when they come down.

- Don't fester in bed until midday, especially if she is getting up with your children.

- Do offer to strip the bed and leave your room tidy.

If you still get a Caroline Bourne-style email after all that, then please tell me what I've overlooked.

The big day

There is so much goodwill going around at weddings, it is astounding that any bad feeling gets an airing; but such is the emotional pitch of celebrations, if there is a lingering unease it will be magnified a hundred fold by the time the bride walks up the aisle. After a good few champagnes and wine at the table, the lid will come off and unfortunately there is no jamming it back on.

You have been warned. Here's a tale of some wedding day MIL madness:

Sally had planned an intimate celebration with just seventy members of her friends and family at a picturesque country house, hidden away in the Lakes.

Neither bride nor groom wanted any fuss; there was no high table, no set speeches – they wanted a relaxed, informal feel to their special day.

Mother-in-law-to-be Marge, having downed more than a few glasses outside on the lawn, had different ideas.

Some of the guests had not yet finished eating when she stood up and dinged her glass with a spoon, calling everyone to attention.

Sally stopped talking and watched, horrified, as Marge launched into her speech.

"She used the entire speech as an opportunity to have a dig at her ex, who was sitting next to her," Sally told me.

"It was all about the fact that he had left them and how her son had been like a husband to her. It was completely humiliating and seemed to go on forever.

"When she finished there was complete and utter silence. Simon had to stand up and clap his hands and say, 'right, everyone, I think we'd better cut the cake'.

"I was so angry. I was absolutely seething. All the time she was talking I was thinking 'sit down, sit down, SIT DOWN!'

"Afterwards she said 'you didn't want me to do that did you?' I just looked at her and said 'well, it's done now, isn't it?' She will still bring it up, even now. I think if she knew it was wrong why did she do it?"

***

Here are some other wedding-related woes, courtesy of DIL:

66 My MIL sobbed when my husband told her he was getting married. It was like bereavement for her. She just couldn't get over the idea of having to share him".

"When my husband told his parents he had met this Bulgarian single mother and was going to marry her they burst out laughing. They honestly thought it was a joke. He had to say, no really, I mean it. There was a deadly silence."

"I showed MIL a picture of the bridesmaids dresses and she said: 'oh no! They're strapless! I thought, oh crikey, my wedding dress is strapless too! What will she think of that! She wanted to be very involved in the wedding planning and then tried to influence all our decisions. I said I wanted balloons on the tables and she said: 'oh, God no. They're so tacky'. In the end I decided the safest way was not to tell her anything about it, if she was going to be critical."

"I remember going to the florist with my MIL before the wedding and I said to the florist that I wanted cornflowers in my bouquet. MIL pulled a face and said 'but I hate cornflowers' and the florist gave me a wink! She'd clearly seen it all before."

"My MIL was very worried people would be getting drunk and vomiting over the tables, so she called our drinks supplier and halved the order without telling us."

"MIL hated me right from the beginning. She rang on the night before the wedding and said how disgusting it was that she hadn't seen my dress yet. My dad went round to see her and told her she was a nasty lady and should apologise."

"My mother-in-law never really got it, when I was getting married. She would say: 'I don't know why you are worried dear, it's only a big party.' Then my sister-in-law got married the following year and it was all bells and whistles all round; no expense spared."

"I remember going wedding dress shopping with MIL, visiting some quite fancy boutiques in London. I'd told her to wear comfortable shoes, as we would be doing a bit of walking. She turned up in a pair of fur-trimmed slippers and said: 'well, you did say comfortable, dear'."

"We decided at the last minute to get out of London and go and visit my fiancé's parents. When we got there, it turned out MIL had arranged to see caterers to do tasting sessions for our wedding without having told us! She was so embarrassed about it, and so she should be! **99**

But don't think MILs are always a destructive wedding day force – here are a couple of tales to warm the heart:

66 My in-laws cut the grass I don't know how many times to get it looking beautiful for our day and did a million other things, without ever reminding us how much they were doing. You have to set aside your petty niggles and remember that they are doing all this, expending time and effort, if not money, trying to do the best for you."

"My MIL was a terrific support throughout all our wedding plans. She knew everything about flowers and cared about all the little details and made sure the whole day was beautiful. It was good for us both to have a fun project in common and gave us loads to talk about. **"**

Good wives

I'd hate to be accused of carping but I'll just come out and say it: it's hard to be a wife these days.

Most of us still feel obliged to assume the traditional role of home-maker, nurturer and all round husband-supporter – if we don't do it, no-one else will.

At the same time, we are bent on career success, whether this is a matter of financial necessity, or because deep down, we believe we will never be truly happy unless we have fulfilled our potential.

Out in the world, like it or loathe it, a woman's worth is very often determined by how she earns her living – the first question at the school gate is "so do you work, then?" – and yet it is mum and not the 'busier', 'more important', less visible dad who will be frowned upon for forgetting a packed lunch or permission slip. "It's not my domain," he'll protest, when asked about dates for kiddies' parties: "Ask the wife".

Your five-year-old is drowning in his brother's massive jumper with his pants outside his trousers? "Oh, that's okay," teacher will giggle, sweetly at the husband, "it's obviously a dad day today".

But if you so much as forget to sign his reading book, she'll freeze right over: "Please, do remember. It's so important to have that continuity with home."

Back at the ranch, many husbands still expect dinner on the table and a clean pair of socks every day (although some women have achieved small victories in getting them to iron their own shirts - other husbands, I hear, even cook a little). Someone has to shoulder the bulk of the dull domestics, however, and it falls, more often than not, to the wife. We screw up all the time, trying to keep it all ticking over and boy, don't they let us know it.

We might start out in our marriage by believing in equality (fools that we are!) – after all, before the kids came along, weren't we still living rather like a couple of students, on an even footing, with similar hopes and dreams for personal and professional achievement?

That all changes as it becomes clear one of us will have to give a little. We look to our mothers and mothers-in-law for enlightenment but reject their dated manifestos with horror; such lives of servitude and forbearance are surely not for us, times have moved on…

And yet they all did it in their day, mostly without complaint. So it's no wonder they suck their teeth at us, for thrashing about in the harness. When held up to MIL's high standards of home-making, I am the ass with my head in the nosebag, slumped in the road, refusing to move.

The wife's role, in this first quarter of the 21st century, remains persistently uncomfortable and undefined. Caught between so many different expectations, we don't even know what to think ourselves, lest of all how to defend our position if challenged by MIL.

We cannot blame her for having high hopes for us, in terms of our wifely capabilities. Wouldn't we put our own children's happiness before all else?

I have a hunch that, if MILs were truly honest with themselves, they would feel reassured if DIL could be persuaded to sign up to something like this on her wedding day:

I, the good wife of (insert name here) do hereby promise to, at all times and without complaint:

-   Keep the house clean and tidy at all times and change my linen often, not just when my children have peed their beds. And to replenish loo rolls and hand towels. (A tea towel just lets you down, dear)

- Plan wholesome meals in advance, sourcing quality ingredients. (MIL did buy you a slow-cooker for Christmas. Have you even plugged it in?)

- Make myself available to my husband should he ever need me to assist him in his **important** work. (Drop whatever you are doing. Reschedule your hair appointment. Cancel your chemotherapy.)

- Never trouble my husband with my shifting moods. (Keep it to yourself, especially if it is about his mother.)

- Instil good manners and behaviours in my children. (This is clearly your job. Your husband will be too busy doing **important** work.)

- Sit with the children through homework and music practice and coach them for exams. (Why do you think your husband did so well at school?)

- Allow him to go to festivals and track days with his mates. (He works so hard, he deserves it.)

- Never nag him about leaving his ties on the floor, or walking over a mopped floor with dirty shoes. (Such trivial matters are beneath him and just poison the air.)

- Never put my own arrangements before the needs of my husband and family. (Your husband is trying to get through to ask for a lift back from the station? Tell your suicidal friend to call the Samaritans instead.)

- Give myself the plate with the gristliest portion of meat on, or the burned bit of crumble.

- Put everyone else's happiness before my own.

(My husband, on reading this, was heard to say: "Yeah, I could get behind that – what's the big deal?")

***

" We can't just have a coffee, when she comes round, we have to have a cafetiere and get all the pretty cups out. If I make her an instant she will tip it down the sink. If we eat cake, we have to have napkins and doilies. If I go to her house I get a chipped mug. Her house is a pigsty and yet she has such high expectations of me – it's like she has all these ideas about the 'perfect' woman she thought her husband ought to have married and she heaps them all on me. I think only a Duchess would have done. She's a complete and utter snob."

"My MIL is always telling me how important it is to keep my husband satisfied. How her friend's husband left her after 68 years because she didn't satisfy him. She'll tell me: 'now it's very important to have regular sex as it keeps you close as a couple. Then she'll say: 'Terry and I ...you know he still sleeps naked?' and I'll cover my ears. **"**

Monster-in-law

Is it ever okay to stop trying?

We were in the middle of DIL Club and as usual, the ladies were
all pitching in with the usual gripes and observations; funnies and
tragedies – all except for one.

This lady sat amongst us, absolutely silently, sipping her drink. She
is a quiet, contained sort of person but I wouldn't have pegged her as
being that shy. Can the rest of us have been too brash for her to bear?
Her silence made me doubt the integrity of the whole project. Perhaps
she thought it wrong of me to hone in on MILs who are only trying to
do their best by us?

Not a bit of it. It transpired that this lady's mother-in-law is so
dreadful that the poor woman – having just endured a two-day
visit - could not bring herself to talk about her. She could barely
string a sentence together, so shaken was she by the exposure to this
impossible, tyrannical matriarch. Our discussions were too close to
the bone for her; she needed a good week's distance from the visit
before she could remember her own name again, let alone form
coherent thoughts.

Several weeks later, my friend opened up about her MIL; how this
woman tears apart the serenity of her domestic set-up, imposing her
will with the force of the Iron Lady. It is not just MILs preposterous,
interfering ways that lay the whole family low, but also her
exasperating lack of tact.

I thought this DIL might be just the person to ask what makes a
truly bad mother-in-law? Also, is there a point where DIL has to say

'enough is enough'? I like to think there is always room for effort but should we every stop trying?

Here is Lana's story, in her own words:

 I've bent over backwards to get on with MIL, for the sake of my husband and children, but she makes it impossible.

She is so judgemental; she made Mark very unhappy when he lived at home, feeling he was never good enough for them. I think now, with me, he has finally seen that it is okay to be himself and they cannot stand that. He is the son who never fitted. It doesn't bother me whether we have my in-laws' approval or not. I just wish they were kind and I do feel sad that my kids don't really know them.

We have tried to encourage her to get to know our children but she doesn't really want to know. She laughs at her friends who help their grandchildren, saying: 'look at poor John down the road, we see him every Tuesday and Thursday pushing that pushchair round the village, poor old bugger'. When we announced I was pregnant, they said: 'don't count on us being doting grandparents'.

What makes a bad MIL? I think it is someone who is unable to step away, or step out and realise how overpowering or crazily restrictive their own behaviour is. It comes down to sensitivity in the end. MIL makes snap judgments about what she finds. If only she could just step back sometimes and not feel she has to do anything about what she sees. I don't mean she can't offer to help, I just mean don't breathe down my neck.

I think there comes a time when you realise you have past the point where you can see how to mend it. After that, you run out of steam and ideas. That's where I am now. I've talked it through with my husband and we've decided that we and our children are the future.

The truth is that his parents are the past. They can join us in what we are creating but they will be left behind if they don't want to fall in with us. Perhaps it might be a comfort for DILs who are unhappy to realise that it is okay for them to focus on the most important thing; yourselves and your family. You are going to grow old with your husband, not your in-laws.

I guess it is sad but I don't see there's anything more I can do. My friends know me as a mediator because of the way I am able to help others. I am quite logical and unsentimental and can help people see things clearly. It is strange to reach this point in my own personal life.

The way forward might be to accept where you are and to try not to make it worse. I could actively cut them off. I would do that if they were malicious. If I discovered they were deliberately trying to harm them I would absolutely do that. We have a polite relationship, no more. I accept that it's not ideal. In a superficial manner, we all manage to maintain that.

My situation is sad but it's not completely broken. These people are doing what they obviously wanted to do. The truth is, if they really cared, when they do have the kids they are intelligent enough to use the time well and get to know them but they make no effort at all.

It's okay, as long as you and your partner accept the status quo. You have to protect yourselves – you can't destroy what you have with your husband over your relationship with his parents. Life goes on, there's no point ruining your life or making yourself miserable over something that won't be here forever – the harsh truth is that they belong to the past. You have to do what you need to do to protect your family's future. **99**

I asked other DILs to identify common failings, as they see them.

This section comes with a noisy caveat: there are obviously some character traits that are more likely to cause problems but I suspect that there are few truly "bad" MILs and that difficulties emerge, more often, from unfortunate clashes of personality.

Selfish...

 She never puts herself out for the kids. They've only ever picked them up once from school. I arrived home and the house was quiet – MIL was sitting having a cup of tea. She'd come home, put the children in the garden and closed the windows and doors. We have a brook at the bottom of the garden that was in flood and I was terrified they might have drowned. They were in their school uniform in the mud with the patio doors closed."

"I used to draw a lot with the kids. Once, I was cooking dinner and we'd got all the pens out. I asked MIL if she would carry on with them and she said: 'Oh no, I don't think so'. She simply doesn't have it in her to make the effort."

Mean...

"My in-laws have this set limit for gifts of £15-£20 no matter what the occasion – it's not because they are struggling to get by. They are well off. For my son's fifth birthday, MIL said she would give us £5 for a cake from M&S. She asked me what he'd like as a present, as well and I suggested a bike helmet, thinking it wouldn't be too much money. She came back to me and said: 'I'm sorry, the bike helmet is £19.50 so we won't be able to buy the cake'."

Interfering...

"My MIL used to drive me to distraction. She would come round just before tea and hand out packets of chocolate buttons to my children, without ever asking if it would be alright. If I tried to protest she'd belittle me in front of the children. Then she'd find fault with my food, as if that was the reason they weren't eating. She'd say something like: 'no wonder they won't touch it, the gravy's all lumpy'."

"I think if you're going to interfere, do something useful like my housework. Stop giving advice. I don't want to know how you breastfed my husband until he was two. Go and dig my garden instead."

Grasping...

"She thinks my husband is the Bank of England. She does everything she can to fill him with guilt, even though he's forever giving her things. She's forever regaling us with stories about her friends' children and how they do so much for their elderly parents. She'll borrow money and then say 'oh, I've got that money I owe you, only I'm going to have to get my teeth done.'"

Grandiose...

"With my MIL, it's all for glory. She will have all her friends round to show off her grandchildren but then neglects them totally. They can be face down in the pond and she wouldn't notice."

Uptight...

"MIL is all about etiquette; she is the kind of person who would send a sympathy card instead of picking up the phone or meeting your eye. She is more like a 2D diagram than a person, or a wooden stick with a nail in the end."

"MIL gets very annoyed over things like not bringing your own towels, or writing thank you cards. I tend to think, fine, send a card the first few times but after that it gets ridiculous. We're all in the same family."

Unrealistic expectations...

"MIL gets hurt when we bring our own travel cot and don't use her ancient, swinging crib, riddled with woodworm or her old high chair with a broken wicker back that would collapse and kill anyone in it and is a real finger chopper to boot. She also takes it as a personal affront if the kids won't eat her food and she'll try to blame me."

Self-absorbed...

"My MIL is a total narcissist. She will do anything if it means she gets more attention, even if it hurts the family. She even made a pass at her old husband in front of his new wife at a father's day dinner we had invited her to. We stopped inviting her to things but she'll turn up anyway and say: 'thank you so much for inviting me'."

Lazy...

"MIL just wants to sit and be waited on. She says she comes to see the children but she just wants to be fed and watered, have a chat and a bit of a social. She likes to monopolise me and neglect the kids."

"They can't be bothered to come and see us. They always expect us to go there. I say 'Ann, you know there are two ends to a motorway'."

Doesn't listen...

"MIL would pay me lip service but never take in anything I was saying. She didn't really want to know, or to get to know me for who I was. She would say 'how's Fiona?' and never 'how are you?', as though she couldn't bring herself to have a real conversation with me. I used to have a few bits of Japanese porcelain on the wall. She'd walk into my house and say, every single time, without fail: 'Oh, those are nice, where are they from?' I thought, 'you're having a laugh'. I wondered whether she was trying to wind me up."

"It is impossible to have a conversation with her as she never listens. I know she has lots of things going on in her head, but it means that I never get through. It makes me feel deflated and unvalued like my opinions don't matter, or that I am too stupid to take seriously."

Simply bizarre…

"My MIL is filthy rich but she is cold as ice. I was in hospital after giving birth; having a cyst removed and my husband couldn't drop the job he was on so we asked his mum to help out. She lasted two days and then said she had to leave as she couldn't cope with the exhaustion.

"When she got back, she sent us a letter with itemised receipts for the ice creams she had bought for the kids and charged us an hourly rate for her time. We also got a list of 'things I would improve about the children's behaviour'. Whenever we visit her she charges petrol when she picks us up from the airport. I think it's a matter of principle. **99**

Taming the beast

"Whoever fights monsters should see to it that in the process he does not become a monster."

FRIEDRICH NIETZSCHE

First things first – keep your claws in, swallow hard and look for higher ground.

Resist the temptation to bite back; count to ten, think about the blocked loo, whatever it takes to stifle the instinctive, aggressive response.

Remember, you have a choice. Your reaction will have a consequence for your relationship and therefore, for the whole family. It is important to stand up for yourself – not to be overborne or intimidated – but this can be done through firm, polite, assertiveness, rather than inflammatory, knee-jerk protest and accusations.

Browbeaten Jenny told DIL Club: "She was being so rude, I just said to her 'there's no need to speak to me like that'. I had taken it for ten years. I wasn't going to let her do it to me any longer."

It must be true that there are truly awful mothers-in-law, just as there are poisonous DILs but there are also coping strategies.

I am a great believer in the redemptive power of emails. Electronic communication is a wonderful tool in maintaining sweet relations with MIL and keeping the monster at bay.

Communicating in person or on the telephone can be difficult if you have little in common, as Claire says:

"If I know MIL is on the phone I will run to the other end of the house, dreading having to talk to her. I have nothing in common with her. She's one of these people who in a conversation gives very little and makes the other person dance around doing all the work."

With emails, however, there are no awkward pauses, no silent judgments, no heightening of tension on the other end of the wire *ie* no messy transfer of power. You remain in absolute charge of the correspondence and you may edit it to perfection, to purge it of anything that might be taken the wrong way and (let's face it, we all do it) to paint yourself and your family in a good light. All she wants to know is that you are all happy, well fed and housed; that her grandchildren are thriving and excelling at school and that you are taking care of her son's emotional and intellectual wellbeing. It's not much to ask.

You know MIL enjoys funny stories about the children – so keep them coming! Tell her about her little grandson crashing great aunty Mildred's disabled scooter into the National Trust tearoom, or how he picked his nose all the way through the nativity.

Even better, send photographs; no-one can take a photograph the wrong way (metaphorically speaking, of course – I am forever in trouble with my husband for holding my iPhone upside down). Wherever you are, whatever you are doing, she will be delighted to see pictures of the grandchildren (unless they are building camps out of her Chelsea Textiles cushions).

Try not to bristle at the curt, instantaneous reply: "What have you done to his hair?!" Choose to take it good spirit. Texts and emails give you the luxury of putting whatever spin on the communication you choose, without worrying about undertones and inflexions.

Sensible DIL Jo absolutely agrees:

66 Communication is definitely the key – if ever we leave it too long, between visits or emails, I always sense a chill in the air; MIL is far more likely to come down hard on us, make negative judgements, or decide we're doing something

wrong. I can hear it in her voice, the moment we ring up.
We feel cross that we are 'in trouble', whereas, in truth, she
is just hurting that she hasn't been more involved with us. **99**

Keeping channels open, however, doesn't mean allowing absolute free flow of information. One cool-headed DIL said she believed it was important to think carefully about the sort of information you impart – or "keep your powder dry", as she put it.

I ask her what she meant; traditionally the phrase, credited to Oliver Cromwell, is to do with trusting in God and conserving your resources but is now understood, more generally, to mean holding something back; in other words, don't go getting all confessional and let everything out, in a bout of verbal diarrhoea.

66 The least MILs know the better. Keep them at arm's
length, that way they have no ammunition to interfere!
I learned this from bitter experience. I realised she was
leaping on every detail and hanging me with it! Things
were much more comfortable when I learned to censor
myself. **99**

She wasn't the only one to have arrived at this conclusion:

66 You do have to protect yourselves. At first I used to be nice
and tell them absolutely everything to keep them in the
loop. Then I realised it was hurting us too much. We were
sinking ourselves. I would send photographs all the time
of the children. I felt that communication must be the key
to success. But they would always turn it back on us and
use it to attack us – criticizing us for taking the children
away so much, or for spending too much time with my
parents. We felt very unhappy and vulnerable. Once we
realised what was going on we decided to keep them in
the dark. It's better now they don't know what we're doing
chapter and verse. **99**

Other DILs also stressed the importance of thinking before opening one's mouth, or hitting send.

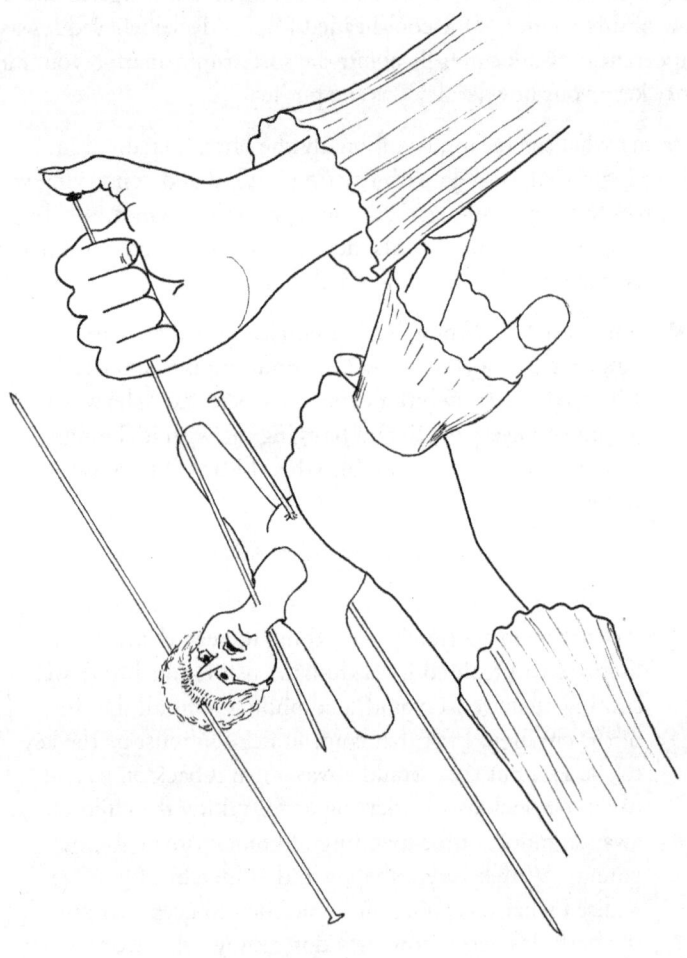

66 It's that thing about not answering in haste but taking the time to think about what you want to say. Don't be reactionary. Put some thought into how you are going to tackle the issue then hopefully you won't end up saying anything hateful and damaging."

"I close the door behind her and have a wobble or rant to my husband afterwards in private but I try not to do it to her face."

"Having a good swear afterwards can be very helpful. My husband and I shut the door after they've gone and say 'fuck off you fucking fuckers'. 99

An interesting solution came in the form of bringing in a buffer; someone to dilute the impact:

66 My MIL is what you might call high maintenance – we describe her as a three-hander sort of a person; she needs someone to entertain her, listen to her gossip or take her out and about and another person to look after her culinary needs and the all vital third to act as a buffer. I slave, my husband regales and we bring in a great aunt to reduce MIL's bossy impact on us all. 99

If in doubt, get out; one of the DILs admitted inventing a book club as a pretext for getting out of the house, whenever MIL visits. She plucks any old decoy book off the shelves and heads for the door.

As a last resort, just leave her to it:

66 Joe's mother always drives everyone insane. Once, we were on the way back from the pub and she'd been going on at me, as usual, when she tripped and fell in a field. Joe said to me 'she'll be OK, just leave her there, we'll go home and put the kettle on.' 99

If you are really brave, you might grab the lion's tail and give it a big tug, just for fun, as these brave ladies did:

66 One Christmas, I bought myself a Mulberry handbag, and got my husband to label it. MIL looked at it and said 'that must have cost a fortune!' like I was bleeding my husband dry. She told me she'd had just the one handbag for the past fifteen years. I said: 'oh, poor you, that's dreadful.' I wanted to really wind her up, so I added: 'Yes, it is fiendishly expensive but you know, I've made a little promise to myself that I'll have a new Mulberry handbag every year.' She just shook her head and looked meaningfully at her husband."

"My in-laws want all of our children to go to posh, English prep schools. MIL particularly hates the Irish and Catholics. I told her that we weren't thinking of boarding school, but that if we were, we would definitely be sending them over to Ireland to go to the big old Catholic boarding school that I went to, where my cousins work and my Uncle is the priest. She went white as a sheet. That's my way of sticking up for myself, by winding her up a bit and showing her that I'm not going to let her dictate to me. **99**

Who's afraid of the big bad MIL?

Once upon a time there were three little girls...

The three little girls grew so big that their mothers said to them, "You are far too expensive for us to keep you here any longer. You must go and find yourselves husbands and set up your own homes. But take care that the big bad MIL does not catch you."

They were good-looking girls and had no trouble at all getting hitched to three brothers who lived over the hill. The husbands, being men, left it to their wives to sort out somewhere to live, so the three little DILs set out together.

Soon they met a man who was carrying some straw. "Please will you give me some straw?" asked first little DIL. "My husband's parents said we can build our own house in their garden."

"Big mistake" muttered the man under his breath, but he sold her some straw at a hugely inflated price and first little DIL kissed him on the cheek.

She got her husband to build it but he failed to lay down any foundations; it didn't even have a front door but first little DIL didn't see the need. They were so in love and with a home of their own, nothing could spoil their happiness.

She said, "now we can have our own space and the big bad MIL will not catch us".

"Poor cow, thought the other two little DILs, whose husbands both worked in the city. "We shall build a stronger house than hers."

Soon they met a man carrying some sticks.

"Please will you give me some sticks?" asked second little DIL. "My in-laws are helping us out with the mortgage, so we can manage at least a couple of bedrooms. MIL wants to be able to come and stay whenever she likes."

"Good luck with that", thought the stick man but he sold her the sticks all the same.

Second little DIL built herself a house out of sticks and it was much stronger than the house of straw – with her husband working away during the week, she thought she could do it all herself but in her haste, she had forgotten to put in any window locks.

She was very pleased with it all the same: "Now we can have our friends round to dinner and the big bad MIL won't catch us and eat us."

"That's what you think," said third little DIL. "I shall build a stronger house than you too."

She walked along the road by herself. Soon she met a man carrying some bricks. "Aha," she thought. "Just what I need. Will you do a discount if I bulk buy?"

"Yes, said the man," and dazzled by her firm handshake and breezy manner, he handed over his best bricks at cut price.

Third little DIL employed the smartest architect in town to design a super secure, comfortable and bespoke house. She emailed the plans to her husband in the city for a second opinion.

"Oh, you clever girl," he said. "You haven't left a stone unturned."

Third little DIL was very pleased with the house and said: "Now the big bad MIL will never get in and if she tries, we'll see her coming on CCTV."

The next day big bad MIL came along the road. She came to the house of straw which first little DIL had built.

When first little DIL saw MIL coming she ran inside her house and pulled the straw across the door. MIL knocked on the door and said "Little DIL, little DIL, let me come in".

"No, no," said first little DIL. "By the hair on *your* chinny chin chin, I will not let you in."

"Then I'll just come in anyway – you're on my land." The big bad MIL marched into the house of straw and ate up her DIL in one swift gulp.

The next day, MIL walked further along the road. She came to the house of sticks which second little DIL had built.

When DIL saw MIL coming she ran inside her house, closed her curtains and jumped into bed.

MIL knocked on the door and said: "For heaven's sakes, I've seen you, now let me in."

"No, no," said second little DIL, pulling her covers up to her chin. "I've told you never to come round without ringing first."

"More fool you for thinking you were ever in charge," huffed the big bad MIL. She climbed through the window, marched through to the bedroom and gobbled up her daughter-in-law, without even taking a breath.

The next day the big bad MIL walked further along the road. She came to the house of bricks which third little DIL had built. "That's a nice house," she thought, "She's got my poor son working himself to the bone to pay for that."

When third little DIL saw MIL coming she ran inside the house, shut the electric gates and turned on the perimeter alarm.

MIL was very angry at this but pretended not to be. She thought: "This one's a clever one. If I want to catch her I must pretend to be her friend."

She buzzed at the gates: "Little DIL, little DIL, I've come with a casserole".

"Thanks but we're getting takeout," DIL buzzed back.

MIL tried again: "I've got tickets for Take That next weekend if you'd like to join me."

"Thanks, but I've got backstage passes already, from work," DIL said.

When MIL heard this she was very, very angry indeed. She was a massive Gary Barlow fan. She growled and whined, gnashing her teeth and running at the gates, which held firm. She tried throwing herself at the wall, but only blunted her claws.

Then, over the intercom, she heard her DIL's voice again: "I suppose you could always come with me, I mean, if you'd like to?"

MIL rolled over and purred like a kitten.

From that day on, MIL switched to a DIL-free diet and dropped in to see third little DIL every Tuesday and Thursday for tea.

Run and hide

(Expelling demons through art...)

It may not always be wise to tell your mother-in-law how you are feeling, especially when those emotions are 'complicated' and may be difficult for her to understand. It can be hard to articulate why you feel the way you do without dealing a mortal blow to the relationship.

Often, such feelings are excruciating for a very short period, until we are able to get them in proportion and rediscover our centre of gravity (or until MIL packs her bags!). It is most unwise to act upon them as they may not be 'real'; they are more likely a knee-jerk response to a (perceived) 'intrusion' fuelled by low self-esteem. Put yourself back in charge and they will vanish without trace.

Of course if you absolutely cannot reassert yourself – you're just not made that way – you will have to rely upon coping strategies that can be trusted to work for you.

One of the women I interviewed for this book expresses her discomfort through poetry; she even admits to hiding away in the bath to exorcise her demons in a notebook, rather than bursting into tears or shouting at her MIL.

It can be very cathartic to expel the bad feeling in this way (better on paper than out in the open) and comes with the added bonus of having created or achieved something, which can always shift a bad mood. Also, concentrating on the task in hand is a great distraction.

Of course, DIL could always run to a quiet corner of the house and read a book – I know plenty of DILs who cope with uncomfortable relationships in this manner. Escaping into a different 'world', rather than the acutely uneasy reality of the present may be an important coping strategy, if you experience these sorts of problems.

Anyway here is Charlotte's poem....

MIL FORCE 12

With a sonic boom she enters a room
A raging gale on the Beaufort scale,
Knocks you flat with the a tip of her hat
Bowls you over, a great steamroller
Stamps on you with the tip of her heel
Grinds you down, at least, that's how it feels.

She turns on you that roving eye and
Woe betides you if you dare lie.
She utters then a raging missive
Look at you flinch! You pale submissive!
Flapping around like a stranded dab,
Unable to speak – have you gone mad?

Surely she'd rather you told her straight,
How she drives you mad...even to hate,
With her pressing need to interfere,
In almost everything you hold dear:
child-rearing, gardening, weaning, times tables,
cooking, cleaning and uniform labels.

It might be fine if you shared her views,
But – you *versus* her – you'll always lose.
There was a time when you had a name,
A job and a life, before she came.
And surely you will again once more,
(Though you doubt it now, that's for sure),
Just as soon as you show her the door,
Your pesky, meddling, mother-in-law.

The hand that rocks the cradle

Child-rearing is a common battleground, especially in the first few years, when new mothers are bombarded with so many alternative ways of doing things.

We tend to read everything to hand, hear the midwives out, listen to mum, MIL and friends and then make up our own minds.

Whether we are on demand feeders or by the clock, bottle or boob, hard-core monitor-free healthy neglecters or co-sleepers; we set up camp – hang out our flag – and dig in for the long haul.

We have to take a position, or we are lost; mired in confusion and sleep-deprived to boot (a woefully unhappy combination).

This is a particularly delicate time and MIL must tread very carefully around the new mother. For example, it is not helpful for her to wade in and begin chafing that baby is desperately dehydrated and needs water ASAP, when the midwife has made it very clear that baby must have colostrum and colostrum only for the first few days.

"Isn't the fontanel sunken?" MIL exclaims, ramming her yellow nails into your precious baby's delicate skull.

"Listen to that pathetic cry! Those midwives don't have the first idea."

You stand back, aghast but powerless as she dribbles boiled water from a teaspoon into baby's mouth.

And yet, on the other hand, she may be right. She truly believes her first grandson is suffering. Do we really expect her not to say anything?

Ladies, if you thought the wedding was emotionally charged, just wait until you have a baby. If MIL and DIL find themselves on opposite sides of the 'big issues', things can get ugly.

Fortunately, my own MIL and I do see eye-to-eye when it comes to most of these subjects. We both share a relaxed, *laissez-faire* attitude to parenting, loosely termed 'healthy neglect'; we don't go for intrusive regulation or anxious, watchful governance. In the early days, I remember MIL saying "happy mum, happy baby" and doing her absolute best to ensure I was well fed (for milk production) and rested. I was very grateful for that. She was also brilliant at swaddling and settling the babies and would take them into her room at the drop of a hat to give me a night off.

I do, however, recall quite clearly the panic that set in as I watched my mother drive away, leaving me with a week-old baby. I sobbed like a Brownie on a sleepover.

No matter how well-intentioned MIL may be, she is not your mother and living under her regime might be something of a culture shock; whereas mum prioritised the overall running of the household, keeping washing and cleaning ticking over, MIL thought those chores were far less important than feeding me up (milk quality control). I remember her cooking up a magnificent feast – more than a week's worth of dishes bubbling on the stove – and me very pettily resenting the resulting mess (onion peels and flour bombs). At the time, I felt that I would rather have had a microwave baked potato than have to clear up.

MILs may also be less astute than our own mothers at picking up on small distress signals; they are oblivious to tell-tale signs of emotional strain – the change of tone, or irritability that would have our mums running for the door. It is a question of sensitivity…

One lady I spoke to said she remembered expressing concern to her MIL that she was not spending enough time with the infant herself (as baby was always in MIL's arms) and was concerned about bonding – to which MIL replied: "Ha! You're worried about bonding! As if he doesn't know where the milk bar is."

The new mother does not understand that children will naturally cleave to and love their mothers; she has read that the period after birth is critical for 'imprinting' this attachment. These are real concerns (in her mind) and should not be dismissed so lightly. Reassurance is what she needs. In other words: give the damn baby back.

New mums cannot be expected to share the confidence and competence of a 60-year-old doyenne with three fully grown children and four grandchildren under her belt. A single, tiny mewling body is all the experience we have and the enormity of that initial dawning responsibility is utterly terrifying.

We are raw as raw can be, emotionally speaking.

I remember hearing a loud bang, followed by a piercing shriek as my baby pulled a wooden shelf on his head, whilst in the care of granny and daddy. Venom coursed through my veins. After all, didn't I look after him 24/7, never taking my eyes off him; 100% safety guaranteed? *Never* on my watch! They have him for two minutes, whilst I am banished upstairs (whether I like it or not), to get some rest and he is damaged, wounded and screaming. I cannot sleep knowing he is in mortal danger. I stamp downstairs and very deliberately prise my child from their grasp, clasp him to my breast and turn my back on them, shooting a deadly glance at my husband. I am horrible; petty, bitchy and prickling. I am a new mother, feeling my way, protecting my own.

These feelings are frighteningly intense. It is a wonder any of us manage to get through those early years without throwing MIL out with the bathwater. Most of us do learn to cope and to rein in our reactionary selves. Here are some tips from sensible DILs:

- Ask her to be sensitive to your needs; this is very difficult. Enlist your husband in balancing his mother's enthusiasm and natural concerns with your need for privacy and peace.

- Recognise the value of a different perspective. Respect her opinion, even if you don't agree. By all means ask for advice; she has been through it all before you. Weigh it all up and decide for yourself.

- Explain, very gently and factually, why you have decided to do things differently but don't always feel you have to justify every little decision. If you know you can't win, don't take her on!

- Smile and carry on doing things as you are. Laugh it off. Constantly justifying yourself might lead her (without realising it) to grind you down as you are allowing yourself to be dominated. It is the psychological equivalent of a land-grab.

- Baby-led weaning? Don't even go there. She won't have heard of it, won't get it, and won't agree with it. Period. Just do it and let her see it in action, once baby has got the hang of it! Expect comments when she sees him gag and drop all of his dinner on the floor but hold firm, if that's how you are doing things. You could give her a book or leaflet; there is plenty of information online.

- As the children grow older, recognise that a grandmother's role is very different from yours; she is not there to discipline. She can get away with a little spoiling and rule-breaking. Just so long as she understands where to draw the line – wrecking your hard-won bedtime routine is definitely on the wrong side of this. All MILs should know that sleep is *everything*.

***

66 When you are a new mum, you are sleep-deprived and very self-conscious and worrying about whether you are a natural mum. I remember feeling very hurt when the baby was screaming and MIL snatched him away saying 'you must be very tired', as though I was unstable and liable to hurt him."

"Kids are the most complicated things that come without instruction manuals. Everyone has to get on, muddling through and doing their best. In my case MIL's was the

loudest voice of all and I didn't find that very helpful. I
wanted to be left in peace to feel my way."

"My MIL was very delicate when I had Sam. She would
send little food parcels and drop them off at the door –
she didn't want to tread all over me as she'd had an awful
MIL herself."

"My MIL refuses to warm up Matilda's lunch. She will say
'just give it to her like that, for goodness sakes'. I have a
good mind, next time she's over for dinner, to give it her
cold and see how she likes it! We used to get on better as I
was always very tolerant and did whatever she wanted me to
do but now I have a baby I can't be like that."

"When my children were babies, MIL would be always
trying to give them honey on everything. I tried to explain
that it is well known that honey can cause infant botulism
but she wasn't having any of it. I came home one day and
caught her dipping the end of his dummy in it. I threw
her out of the house and told her it was clear that she had
no respect for me."

"When MIL came to see the baby for the first time, she
arrived ridiculously early, piled high with gifts from a
stack of people I had never heard of. She insisted I reply
in full to each and every one of them with written thank
yous. She is all about protocol, before all else."

"When I told MIL we were having twins she said 'it's great
you've got your mum and dad and friends to help' but
didn't once suggest she might chip in."

"MIL has an opinion on everything to do with my children
and she has never learned the art of keeping it to herself.
She doesn't realise what young people get up to nowadays.
She has very fixed ideas from a completely different
generation."

"I think MIL needs to remember that it's not her baby. She's done her bit, now it's DIL's turn. She should take her cues from DIL and keep her tongue. On DIL's side, she should listen to everything, make up her own mind and do what comes instinctively – and not feel that she has to argue about or justify everything all the time."

"I remember when I was a brand new mum I went shopping with MIL in Birmingham. Everything I tried on, she would say: 'Don't worry, that's not for you at the moment. Six months down the line and you'll be back to normal.' I came away with nothing. I hated her for that. She was much more anxious for me to get my figure back than I was. **99**

Damned if she does...

So it seems our MILs simply cannot get it right; if they try too hard to please they annoy us. If they are 'hands-off', they are selfish and uninvolved. If they are too involved they are interfering and overbearing.

Were there any kind of real love underpinning the whole affair – or real friendship of any kind - then of course we would forgive them their foibles. The cruel truth is that, for many DILs, they would rather not have MIL around. Including her in family life is mere duty; there is no pleasure in it, sometimes quite the contrary. MIL's visits can shake the foundations of the family unit and strike terror into the heart of the fledgling wife. Why should we put our heads on the block?

MIL might do all the right things – put herself out for us in the most selfless and giving fashion – and yet we still find it impossible to play nice, particularly where there is no sympathetic chemistry between us.

This is mean-spirited ladies, it really is. She raised and nurtured your husband; without her, your children would not exist. I am afraid it is quite simple. You owe her. Confucian notions of filial piety apply (stopping short of sacrifices after her death). She deserves your consideration, respect and support.

When taken together, *en masse* and displayed as a litany of grievances, it becomes very clear just how whimsical our complaints sometimes are:

Helping too much...
66 They'll march in the kitchen and go through my cupboards, helping themselves. I think they need to realise

that, to you at least, they are strangers and they need to observe some sort of protocol."

"It's hard for them to accept we are capable adults. MIL always has to bring me a casserole but there is that element of a suggestion that I don't know how to cook. She'll ring me three weeks in advance and say 'now, would you like me to make a crumble?' I think I don't know what the bloody hell we're going to eat tomorrow let alone in a month. Don't go bothering me about crumbles."

"They will say 'we'd like to bring a crumble but we don't want to offend you', or 'we'll bring our own duvets and pillows as we know how busy you are'. I know they're doing their best but it gets on my nerves. I can feel myself bristling. MIL even brought her own self-inflating bed once."

"She comes in the house and takes it upon herself to do our washing. She once shrunk a beautiful silk camisole and knickers that my fiancé, as he was, had given me. She presented me with these Barbie-sized pants, without a word of an apology. I was in tears! She never said sorry. We just don't refer to it."

"I know I shouldn't moan – we couldn't survive without my in-laws – but I can't help it!" **99**

Not helping enough...

66 They sit there like guests in my house waiting to be offered a cup of tea. When I say 'you could have helped yourself', they'll tell me they didn't like to look in my kitchen cupboards. I mean, what do they think I might have in there? A rampant rabbit?"

"When we had our first baby I think MIL was so keen to leave us in peace she stood right back and did nothing at all. It would have been nice if she'd made the odd dinner and brought it round."

So we moan like stink when MILs stick their noses in, but they can also get under our skin by trying too hard not to interfere:

66 My MIL had had such an interfering Mil herself, she was ever so worried about upsetting me. It was like getting blood out of a stone asking for her help or advice. I asked her to help with flowers for our wedding but she said it wasn't really her thing. I think she didn't want to tread on my toes or mess it up for me. She was massively over-compensating."

"My MIL is quite good at keeping things to herself and trying not to interfere but sometimes you can see she's trying so hard, she tiptoes around me and I find it very annoying. She's very nice, I know I am frequently horrible to her and she doesn't deserve it."

"She'll hover in the kitchen, asking if there is anything she can do. I can sense how nervous she is around me and try to be nice but inside I am pure evil. All I want to say is 'get out!' **99**

A very strange habit

Marge has a very particular way of eating her fruit corners. She has one every day of her life, except Sundays and has been eating them for the past 20 years; a grand total of 6,240 yoghurts, if DIL's maths is correct. The cherry ones are the best. Marge ought to know.

If you've ever seen her eat one, you won't forget it in a hurry. She has her own unique style. When DIL first experienced it, she could not look away. She sat, transfixed, hypnotised almost and just a little bit horrified, until the very end.

First Marge gets stuck into the lid with her cavernous mouth and leathery, white tongue. Don't sit too close, or you'll get a waft of something unpleasant.

She licks it clean in a matter of seconds; most of us do that (except for thin people, who never lick yoghurt lids), you say, but then most people stop there. Not Marge.

Marge starts on the pot itself, using her tongue to work her way around the rim, making little sucking noises. She will perform extraordinary contortions to excavate the corners, craning her neck at impossible angles and letting out the odd grunt.

She uses her thumb to wipe out every last smear, scratching away until she has scoured the pot clean.

At last, she settles back into the sofa, with the empty pot and spoon balanced on her tummy, turns on the news and promptly falls asleep.

***

If MIL has a peculiar habit, however, chances are it will get under DIL's skin and become a source of irritation.

Here are a few of the things that poor MILs do that drive their daughters-in-law to distraction:

66 My MIL is so messy – she will come in and within minutes the sides are covered in her rubbish. Now we have a sideboard in the hall by the back door just for her mess. I'd like to go to her house and tip my shopping all over her side."

"Her idea of tidying up is the scrape the breadboard into the sink, dump teabags on the side and sweep crumbs on to the floor."

"When she annoys me I try to remember that I am probably annoying her too. I like everything to be organised and structured – I know how different I am to her in that respect. I'm sure she thinks I'm over the top."

"If she can't find something in her handbag she just empties the whole thing out and it all goes flying across the room and we have to bend down and help her put everything back in."

"When MIL does the ironing she turns everything inside out. I have to go through it all and turn it the right way round. It takes me forever and drives me mad."

"She always arrives with her clothes in a washing basket, even though she has loads of cases. She just can't be bothered – and she always says to me: 'What must you think of me?' She can never find anything in it. When my husband sees his own parents coming up the drive with that basket he'll say: 'just look at the state of them!'"

"She will never let Jim (her partner) write anything on her calendar. She insists he keeps his own one. Then of course she forgets to write on it, so he never knows what

he's supposed to be doing from day-to-day. It's always a mammoth task to arrange anything with either of them."

"She insists on using one towel between the two of them, so as not to dirty our linen but then she uses it for absolutely everything, including mopping the bathroom floor so it gets absolutely disgusting!"

"She has this address book but never writes anything in it in alphabetical order. If you need a number she'll say: 'oh, he's the one to the left of the coffee stain'."

"My MIL has this habit, whenever we go out for a meal, of waiting to see what I'm going to have and then copying it. I suppose it might be a form of flattery but it drives me mad. It ends up in a bit of a competition – who can hold out the longest. I now say: 'Oo, I don't know. I haven't quite decided, there's so many lovely things on the menu and try to outwait her."

"My MIL pronounces parmesan 'par-mee-san'. I don't know why it should bother me but it does. I think sometimes she does it on purpose."

"If MIL put sugar in her tea she always bangs the side of the cup as she stirs it, round and round. It's like a bell ringing and besides, it's very bad manners.

99

Killing with kindness

"We are all formed of frailty and error; let us pardon reciprocally each other's folly - that is the first law of nature."
(Voltaire: Dictionnaire Philosophique)

Sometimes, trying too hard to be nice is enough to push DIL over the edge.

It might be that she sees MIL's actions as encroachment upon her turf. Or she could be too busy to fully process whatever it is that MIL is trying to do for her and has no energy for gratitude, especially when the good deed was unsolicited. Or, she may register that MIL is being over-generous and feel uncomfortably guilty. Or it may just rub her up the wrong way, for reasons no more logical than a simple personality clash.

Some DILs will take offence when MIL arrives with a casserole. They take it as a personal slight; an implication that they are not capable of providing for their own family and will accept it less than graciously. Other DILs might lose it when they are offered a cup of tea for the tenth time in one day. There is no apparent justice in these reactions – we are in the wrong here, ladies.

We must not underestimate the hurt that in-laws feel when their actions – which are only borne out of love and kindness – are met with rejection and ingratitude.

Often MILs are guilty of trying too hard to help; they want so much to be the magic fairy that waves her wand and erases any struggle from our lives. We appreciate this, we absolutely do – objectively and rationally (what parent would not want to ease their child's burden?) – but emotionally we sometimes resent it.

We feel squeezed out, inadequate, incompetent, disempowered and above all, guilty that she has stayed up until the early hours doing something for us that we should very well do for ourselves, like taking up curtains; or arranging for a plumber to fix a problem that should have been sorted months ago.

Her actions immediately set her on higher ground, although this is not her intention; she is the noble, beneficent homemaker (and let's face it, the grown-up) and we are the ungrateful children, muttering thanks that can never match up.

This can tap into a deeper moral guilt about our extravagant, spoiled generation and nudges us perilously close to the edge – all over a pair of curtains, or leaky radiator. It is ridiculous. Removed from the acute discomfort of the moment we can get things in proportion and even laugh about it – but it is a powerful psychological subtext and a wrecking ball to our delicate relationship.

We try to relax and accept help but we're just not wired that way. We are tense, edgy, over-sensitive and tremendously awkward, or 'off-centre'. We want to scream, 'Look at my family – do they look malnourished? How do you think I cope when you aren't here? Give me some credit for having fed and raised them for nearly a decade!' Our in-laws do not deserve this response and we feel cross with ourselves – and immature – that we cannot put these feelings aside.

This is clearly a subjective response, dictated by certain personality types and upbringings; some DILs might say they would love to have MIL do everything for them. I am certain, however, that we all need to struggle a bit, now and again – and that our pride, dignity and sense of self-worth depend upon it. Doing things for us that we ought to do for ourselves is, ultimately, disempowering. MILs need to understand that we may have different priorities and standards – we will do things in our own time. They must not jump in and grab the reins. If we want to live with sockets hanging out of the walls and curtains dragging in puddles of cat wee, then that is our prerogative.

The question remains: how to decline offers of help, without causing offence?

***

My good friend Jan has some sensible advice:

66 Channel the good intentions and make them work for you. My MIL used to arrive with loads of horrible cakes and cheap sweets (we don't let the kids eat sweets). I think she's trying to make up for the fact she doesn't get to see them that often. I want to say 'right Pat come on in, there's the bin'.

Instead, I've said to her, very gently – 'Pat, what was that lovely ham you did for us last Christmas? Do you think perhaps you could do one of those for us next time you come?' Now she just brings the ham. **99**

I have another friend who gives her MIL recipes that she would like made up, at stressful times, such as a new birth. These are verbal contracts if you like – unwritten rules that help define the parameters of 'assistance' and prevent it from spilling into 'interference'.

There is a fine line; some MILs ride a chieftain tank through the boundaries and keep on going, firing all the time. It is up to us to remind them, very delicately, where those boundaries lie and also, perhaps, why they are important to us.

66 They bring out that ridiculously over-dependant streak in me. If my own mum said 'can I bring a pudding on Sunday?' I will say 'that would be great', but if MIL says it, I will say 'no, thanks, I'm fine'."

"Some people feel affronted if MIL is doing things like that for them but I am certainly not too proud to accept the help. I couldn't survive without her."

"I'm not too proud if someone wants to go shopping for me. I know some people might take that as a criticism."

"MIL came to my house when I was in hospital and said 'I hope you don't mind but I've done a little bit of cleaning … not that I thought your house was dirty'. Oh, my God, that was the best present I've ever had but I know my sister-in-law would be offended by that. When MIL mopped her kitchen floor she almost threw her out. I think it depends whether you think she sees you as a grown-up and equal or as a child, like her son. If you don't feel respected then your hackles will go up. That's not a good relationship."

"My MIL was a wound up bundle of trapped energy; I just had to learn to channel that by giving her tasks. She was like a firework in a bottle with the stopper down. Energy removal solved the problem. **99**

Paranoia

"Fear is the path to the dark side. Fear leads to anger. Anger leads to hate. Hate leads to suffering."

Yoda (Star Wars)

Sally's mother-in-law is a formidable character. She is so astute, so acutely perceptive that just one glance, one searing blaze of her sharp green eyes can reduce Sally to a jabbering wreck. The light penetrates every dark corner of her soul and she registers every weakness, every last foible. MIL sees *everything*. Sally stands before her in judgment and is inevitably found wanting.

Of course this is all in Sally's head. Paranoia is a prime threat to the MIL-DIL relationship; it muddies the waters and if left unchecked, will make honest, open communication impossible.

An over-sensitive DIL will always be on the alert for possible criticism, whether real or imagined. She will see MIL's involvement in her life as questioning even the most trivial of her decisions. She lives in fear of judgment.

Even when MIL couldn't give a fig about the choices her DIL has made, a sensitive DIL views herself through her MIL's eyes and measures herself against imaginary criteria. She foists on her MIL all manner of principles and credits her with opinions which might be entirely fictitious.

This is a debilitating way to live; if DIL continues to feed this demon (*ie* her paranoia) on her shoulder it will undermine everything she does.

The demon will cling on to a wisp of a comment and whip it into a full scale attack on DIL's housekeeping, her parenting style, her culinary instincts … or whatever the issue of the day happens to be. She won't find the demon applauding a fluffy baked alaska or chirping over a brilliant school report. He perches in sardonic revelry, rocking with joy at DIL's uncomfortable parents' evening and cackling at her soggy sprouts.

If you are a DIL who suffers from such negative feelings, perhaps it would be helpful to de-personalise comments and try not to feel slighted. Stop and think whether you would feel so strongly if someone else had said the same thing. Learn to trust your MIL and give her the benefit of the doubt that she may not have meant it in the way you have interpreted it.

Above, all, you must absolutely let things go when you wave MIL off; do not give these feelings currency in your daily lives and try not to let them poison your relationship with your husband.

Unfounded or excessive fears can be very dangerous. They can morph into an irrational mistrust of MIL's intent and delusions of persecution. They can grow, out of all proportion and do real damage to relationships – DIL might tell herself that they are grounded in logic and reason but the chances are that she has lost the ability to think clearly.

She needs to find a more rational standpoint, to recover her equilibrium and clear-sightedness. It can be extremely difficult to do this from the inside of a relationship, where there is little objectivity. Where these feelings interfere persistently in the relationship (and particularly if this is not the only problematic interpersonal relationship in DIL's life) DIL may need to seek professional help from a counsellor or behavioural therapist.

DIL shouldn't beat herself up for having these feelings in the first place. Everyone suffers from the odd paranoid delusion; the trick is to get them back under control before they take over.

***

66 It's taken me a long time to understand that MIL won't or can't change at her age - but that I can change the way that I react to her. Now when she says 'oh, surely he should be eating lumps by now?' I just smile and say that it is not for the want of trying."

"I think you have to learn to put yourself in her shoes. Nine times out of 10 she's not being malicious. You need to take a moment and think "hang on, I don't honestly think she's trying to piss me off here".

"I'm not sure sometimes whether I'm being paranoid or not. I hear her slagging other people off all the time and I think that she must be like that about me when I'm not there."

"I think it all comes down to trust. If she behaves in a way that makes you feel secure – that it is okay to be you and that you are good enough for her and her son, then you are less likely to torture yourself with negative thoughts. If she constantly undermines you, through little comments – trivial though they might seem when taken in isolation – then no wonder you begin to self-destruct. Of course, the trick is not to care so much. Her opinions shouldn't matter. They belong to the past."

"It often depends on my own mood – how I react to her. If I'm feeling a bit low, I can take everything the wrong way."

"Don't filter what you hear through your biases. People sometimes hear what they want to hear."

"His mother was dreadful – I would try to have a conversation with her and she was always so standoffish. I went hand over fist to try to get on with her. She was one of those women who would sit drinking and smoking in the corner, looking like she'd swallowed a wasp. After we'd broken up I remember her coming into the pub where I worked. She stayed there for most of the day. At the end she was sobbing into her glass: 'You and Jim were so good together...' I literally couldn't believe it. It just shows that you can never tell what people really think - yet we base so much of our own behaviour on what we think other people are thinking! **"**

The art of receiving

"Dear Valerie,

Thank you so much for the size 20 pyjamas. Happily, I've lost quite a bit of weight since the birth and am now back into my old jeans (size ten, for the record). I wondered if you might get some use out of them?

Much love,

Fiona"

There is an art to receiving unwanted gifts from MIL; it's quite simple – you thank her, graciously, act delighted with the toe-nail clippers, or cold cream for ageing skin and then put them in the present cupboard, for re-gifting.

What you must NOT do, is interpret the gift as some sort of hidden message, or Trojan horse. This is most unlikely – the idea of MIL, chewing her pencil, conjuring up the most pointed gift to buy you, just to needle you, is a paranoid delusion.

Isn't it much more likely that she is trying to find something truly practical, as befitting your needs? Massive pyjamas? Well, they're just more comfortable, aren't they, particularly when you're recovering from a C-section. Face cream for ageing skin – it's just face cream to her. She left her glasses behind and couldn't read the small print. Or she was in a hurry and simply clutched at a recognisable brand. Why would you torture yourself with notions of villainy? It's just not helpful.

Even if she did intend a barb, surely it is better to ignore it and pretend you have missed the point?

I very much enjoyed hearing about some of the surprising gifts daughters-in-law have been lucky enough to receive from their MILs:

" I was serving out in Afghanistan and I happened to tell my husband how difficult it was to get anything clean. The next thing I knew, I received a big package. When you're in the forces, if ever someone sends a parcel out from home, it's quite a big deal and everyone gathers round to see what you've got, including your superiors. They were all silent whilst I battled with all the brown tape, then burst into great whooping and whistling as I produced the most enormous bag of disposable paper knickers from my mother-in-law! That was all there was. I was so embarrassed; I turned bright red and ran out of the room. I know she meant well – it was quite sweet really – and she would have had no idea that they would have gone down like that."

"We were all sitting round last Christmas and my husband was giving out the presents. He handed me one from my MIL and I must admit I thought, Oh God, what's it going to be? Last year I got engine oil. Well, I opened it in front of everyone and pulled out some nasal hair clippers. I couldn't look her in the face. My kids were all going 'mum, what's it for? Can I have a go?' I just shoved it under my pile and muttered a quick 'thank you'. She clearly thinks I've got a problem!"

"For my 30th birthday, my MIL bought me chin hair removal cream."

"I was lucky enough to get 'Insolence', the perfume."

"The best one ever was a part-used bottle of old perfume. She's now my ex-MIL."

"She bought us a mattress for a wedding present because she said she'd got it cheap."

"Every Christmas, all the DILs in the family got exactly the same gift, like she wasn't prepared to recognise us as individual people. One year it was a sewing basket, presumably so we could all darn our husbands' socks."

"My MIL worked as a GP and quite often got lots of presents from patients at Christmas. One year she'd obviously re-gifted some chocolates, which she might have got away with if she'd been bothered to take off the label. I got 'Dear Doctor, thank you - my son's acne has all but cleared up now", from a Mrs Cartwright."

"She'll give me £100 a year for the children and then say, very pointedly, 'well, I don't get to see them and buy ice-creams like other grandmas, do I?'"

"She rings to ask what my son would like on his birthday and says 'you get the present and I'll pay you back'. Why doesn't she phone him up herself and ask him? He's not a baby any more. She won't even ring them on their birthdays. She'll say 'oh, well, last time we rang he didn't sound as though he really wanted to speak to us'. I think 'he's a child, for goodness sakes.'"

"My in-laws always send down presents for the children at half-term – already labelled, with 'do not open until December 25th'. I don't want presents at half-term, I want them to get up off their lazy backsides and come and see us at Christmastime. It's as though they get nose bleeds north of Bristol."

"I was quite newly pregnant when we went to see MIL, on my birthday. We were having tea when she said 'hang on; it's your birthday isn't it? Wait here, I've got something for you'. She went upstairs and came back with this size 18, black linen dress. She said 'you'll need this when you get really big over the summer – I bought it for myself but I don't really like it'. I was so insulted I went home, screwed it up and put it in the bin.

99

Micromanagement

"Don't think I'm interfering, but…"

Some MILs really cannot help themselves; they stand on our threshold correcting the tiniest of details in our domestic order.

In business, such an approach is generally considered as destructive and harmful to morale and productivity (in the extreme, it can impinge upon employee physical and mental health).

The same might be said of a marriage.

Tell-tale signs of micromanagement are identified as:

- Finding it difficult to delegate work

- Discouraging others from making decisions without being consulted

- Constant monitoring and requesting unnecessarily detailed reports

- Disregarding experience and knowledge of workers

- Focusing on wrong priorities

- Demotivation of team

The problem most commonly arises when there is a lack of trust and confidence, such as manager working with a new or unfamiliar team. Or, the manager may be behaviourally dependent upon control over others. Do I have to spell out the obvious parallels here?

Where MIL is guilty of micromanagement, the result can be toxic. DIL has no breathing space in her own home and the marriage runs out of air; either that or DIL and hubby join forces and throw MIL out on the street.

Interfering in-laws are said to be responsible for as many as one in ten marriage breakdowns in the UK (as of June 2013), according to a study by the Co-Operative Legal Services. A Netmums poll of 2,000 women in 2011 found that almost a quarter would describe their relationship with their MIL as 'bad or terrible'. The most common complaints were that MILs were 'judgemental, controlling and interfering'. A high proportion of the Netmums respondents (24%) said that they found managing relations with MIL as stressful as moving house.

I do think MILs are prone to make snap judgements, especially where contact with DIL's family is limited. They will leap on small details and extrapolate – too many beans on a plate equals persistent overfeeding, or a sharp reprimand in front of MIL signals over-fussy and restrictive parenting (and yet a failure to chastise a child for

leaving the table without asking must be evidence of sloppy discipline).

Living under such scrutiny, we see it even where there is none; our hackles go up over the tiniest morsel of advice.

We feel we are on show at all time and vulnerable to attack and misinterpretation. MIL's eyes seem to follow us around the room like the Mona Lisa, scrutinising our every move.

MIL should learn to keep her counsel – she should wise up and bite her tongue – but this is not a book about managing DIL. We can't change MIL. We have to learn to ignore these little 'digs', as we see them, or make light of them, robbing them of the power to wound or agitate.

***

66 I know that the first thing she'll do when she gets in the door is an inspection. I will be on my hands and knees all day, with a rag, barking at the kids for dropping crumbs. She'll go straight to the windowsill and say 'don't worry, you'll get around to wiping all the flies off eventually'."

"When we moved into our new house we had to do everything to it. My MIL had an opinion on everything; taking up the floorboards, rewiring, you name it. Without fail, whatever we'd decided, she would say: 'I wouldn't do it like that…' In the end we went against her advice and it caused a massive family rift. We haven't spoken since. I know it is a shame and I feel bad about it but really it's more their loss than ours."

"Whenever MIL comes over at tea time, without fail, she'll look at what they're eating and tell me off for giving them too much on their plate. It drives me mad!"

"My husband was going on a business trip once and I was packing his bag. She came and leant over my shoulder and said 'not like that, the shirts will get all creased'. She stood right over me and watched me do it until I had finished."

"I said I would get tea for the boys, which was unusual in itself as when she's around she always likes to do it. I was heating up a pan full of water and I could feel her eyes watching me around the kitchen. She came over and looked in the pan and quite literally told me how to boil an egg. She has no idea she's even doing it, or of the effect it has."

"My MIL will come over and look in my wardrobe and tell me off for being a hoarder. Just because she hasn't been near the shops in ten years."

"My MIL is brilliant. The last thing she wants to do is interfere. She'll say to me: 'Don't ask me for advice – you can ask me and I'll tell you what I did but don't take it as gospel. **"**

Facebook faux pas

"Facebook should have a breathalyser attached!"

"Try as hard as I might, I just can't bring myself to 'like' her updates."

"MIL wanted to arrange something with me and tried to do it on a comment thread about something totally different. I wrote back *'IM me'* – to which she replied *'of course you are!'"*

Facebook is a complicated social engineer. On its good side, it is all about connecting people, rekindling old friendships, building communities online and reassuring us that we are not alone in this cruel world.

But it is a two-faced friend; the other side indulges murkier intentions, allowing us to spy on other people's lives turning everyone we know into characters in our own, tailor-made soap.

We creep around like voyeuristic snoops in a virtual society, proclaiming against the show-boaters and obsessive status updaters with full-blown hypocrisy and withholding our likes, just to spite. I'd doff my cap at Mary Whitehouse and venture that there is something quite distasteful about the whole business.

MIL and her generation stick out like sore thumbs in this social network. They are unlikely to find their own way in, for starters. They generally deem it a waste of time; they just don't get it and don't see the need to expend mental energy figuring it out. The odd one or two elderly aunts who do pop up in comments below other friends' status posts strike us as freakish kinks in the system.

Enter your mother-in-law to the FB party; but remember that once invited you cannot take it back. Who would ever 'unfriend' their MIL and not expect to live to tell the tale.

Be ever so careful in those halcyon, carefree, love-fuelled, rose-tinted early days, when MIL is brimming over with gratitude towards you for taking him on and you are deferential and eager to please, linking arms and sharing chocolate oranges over *X Factor*. Don't, whatever you do, allow all that super good feeling and warm tingly-ness to spill over into an *actual Friend Request*. Or, if you do, pause a minute to think it through before you click.

Once she's in, she'll see everything you post, forever more. Not only your posts but your tags – remember that photo of you stroking the Butler in the Buff at a friend's hen do? Or that one of you pretending to snog your best friend after Gemma's wedding? That thread where you and your spinning class mates were slagging off your husbands?

Do you want her to see you as you really are? Do you think you – or she – can cope with that?

Don't most wives spend their married lives playing the role that we think the previous generation expects of us? The pinny-wearing, jam-kettling, chutney-brewing supermum? Surely it's our job, above all, to protect from the real truth?

You should be particularly careful if you are one of those Facebookers prone to confessional status updates – do you want her dropping on your online admissions of hangovers, of missed deadlines, forgotten bookbags (again), general tardiness and some-time bitchiness? She will see you in a whole new light.

She'll tune in to you sharing with friends your love of *TOWIE*; how you record and replay *The Real Housewives of Beverly Hills*; you just love those alabaster busts and marble roll-tops. Do you want your MIL to know that you are THAT SHALLOW? It rather undermines your spectacularly good (if heavily borrowed) contribution to the in-laws' discussion of Syria last Sunday.

Think people, what you are getting yourselves into, that's all.

Of course, your MIL might be a technophobic luddite, who winces at the mere mention of Facebook: "I know you set me up on that once, dear, but I've never found myself again".

Phew! You dodged a bullet there. Long may it continue. Just beware peppy old Barbara from choir, who has her own FB page on medieval manuscripts and a friends group of 300 plus ex-anthropology students. Make sure she doesn't sidle up to MIL with her iPhone at choir coffee break, and let her back in.

❝ My MIL is on Facebook but she doesn't get it that everyone can see her status updates. She usually gets on it late at night after a few glasses of wine and starts ranting, usually about me, or how she doesn't see her grandchildren enough! Lucky for me she hardly has any friends. I just ignore it. She'll be texting me again the next morning, like nothing has happened."

"My husband once made me supper in the shape of a large phallus – long piece of salmon, two new potatoes and lots of humus were involved - and because we were fairly well oiled we thought it was HILARIOUS so I posted a pic on FB forgetting my MIL was friends with me. Well she was fairly disgusted with the picture, but it was the floodgate of comments about my husband's past misdemeanours that really got her goat - there were many stories about his drunken antics; wetting beds, getting arrested for indecent exposure - it was all there in the comment thread! She saw her beloved son in a whole new light. Facebookers beware!"

"My MIL asked if we could be Facebook friends and I turned her down, right away. I made a joke about it, saying I didn't want her seeing all my embarrassing pictures, but really I was thinking 'fuck, no!' ❞

The Honeychurch taint

"Yes, but she is purging off the Honeychurch taint, most excellent Honeychurches, but you know what I mean." – Mrs Vyse, Lucy Honeychurch's mother-in-law, to her son Cecil.

E.M. FORSTER, A ROOM WITH A VIEW

There may very well be things MIL would like to change about you, but if she's got any sense, she'll keep them to herself.

You will have a happier relationship with MIL if you can manage to preserve your own identity; try not to let MIL impose her expectations, views or values upon you. By all means listen to them and deal with them respectfully and politely but don't feel you have to espouse them lock, stock and barrel. Just because she may be forceful in expressing them doesn't mean she expects you to trade-in your old opinions and values for hers. Who would do that? That would be weird.

If you really believe that MIL is trying to change you – to 'improve' you, or influence your fundamental beliefs or outlook – be prepared to admit that it could be a sign of paranoia.

When MIL says, "Oh, you give the egg seven minutes? I always do it for six," she is not questioning your abilities as a cook. If she comments: "I never wear horizontal stripes", she is not suggesting that you should throw away the sweater you just bought because it makes you look fat. She is merely stating facts, or talking off the top of her head without thinking it through.

Even if it were true – she does think you look fat - why should you care? Wear it if you like. Take her advice on board if you choose. It is your decision. BE A GROWN-UP.

If you are a devout church-goer and MIL buys you a copy of Christopher Hitchens' polemic *God is Not Great* for Christmas, you don't have to read it. She is trying to engage you in critical debate, not pull the rug from under you, or plunge you into psychological trauma. Be flattered that she thinks you can take it.

Don't take everything as a critique of your failings, or as questioning your most fundamental make-up. You have to learn to be secure in yourself so that this sort of stuff can't wobble you.

The trouble is, if you are a chameleon (the modern word, I am told, is 'morph') – that is if you adapt to whatever social setting you find yourself in – then you do tend to lose sight of yourself. It is hard to be secure in what you think and feel about anything when you are constantly measuring yourself against others:

> When lacking a sense of their own inner needs, such superficial extraverts may end up (despite their charm) as rootless chameleons, endlessly taking their social cues from other people...
> Daniel Goleman, *Emotional Intelligence* (London 1996)

Morphing is a particularly modern concept, in an era when so many of us are dislocated, geographically and culturally from our roots; moving up and down social strata without primer or guidebook. The whole thing can be quite bewildering for someone who is wired to bend themselves to the system, rather than vice-versa.

Lifted into an alien environment – out of her comfort zone – DIL might feel as though she is scratching around in the props cupboard, with the lights out; she's not even sure which costume she's looking for. For some DILs this is not merely disconcerting, it can be quite terrifying. DIL might strive to avoid such situations wherever possible – avoiding visits to the in-laws, or not picking up the phone if she suspects MIL may be on the other end – out of real fear, that she might not be 'good enough'.

I often think this must have been how Princess Diana felt, losing herself, or rather her sense of self, in the opulent surrounds of

Kensington Palace. She may have had blue blood and been to a fancy finishing school but she was working as a playgroup assistant and casual cleaner when she was plucked from normal life and dropped into a palace.

Andrew Morton's controversial biography of Princess Diana – *Her True Story* – painted a picture of a woman suffering under the oligarchical regime of the Royal Family and forced to bow to 'the firm' in all things. She cracked under the strain; her unhappiness allegedly found expression in bulimia and hysteria.

Far be it from me to comment on the Queen as mother-in-law – I wouldn't risk a disembowelment – but Diana's experience, extreme though it is, might serve as a potent reminder of the need to retain a strong sense of self within your new family unit. You have to learn to trust your mother-in-law and try to relax in the knowledge that being yourself will be good enough for her.

Under my husband's influence I am sure I must have changed and taken on some of his behaviours – it is inevitable after ten years of marriage. Some of those changes will be for the better; I now leave a full 15% tip in restaurants, instead of a bit of loose change. But I still cannot send back drinks when a waitress has got our order wrong and I will never be able to find my car keys without swearing and breaking into a sweat.

My point is that we all need to feel that we are okay as we are; that we are 'good enough', despite all of our foibles and imperfections.

It might help DIL to focus on the positive things she has brought to the family; a love of music and concerts, perhaps, or an interest in baton twirling and herpetoculture. Her interests and personal qualities cannot fail to have enriched the family as a whole. There must have been something about her that made her husband want to marry her in the first place.

***

66 "My MIL is like the Queen. The power she has over everyone in the family is ridiculous. It's like a vortex and you can get pulled in. You don't realise how dangerous it can be."

"It is clear to me that MIL thinks I am not good enough for her son. With her, everything is about social status and I don't make the cut. I would never have imagined we would end up having problems like this. It goes against the grain for me as a person not to get on with someone. It makes you have negative feelings about yourself. As soon as she walks in the room I find myself muted. I just can't talk. Simon says 'why aren't you saying anything?' I can't help myself. I retreat into a shell. People who know me socially wouldn't believe I could be like that. My friends say, look Amy, you're nearly forty, why should you care? At some point, you have to protect yourself, or it is not healthy."

"My MIL is like Hyacinth Bucket. We go to posh places to eat but nothing is ever good enough for her. No wonder she gives me such a hard time."

"My MIL just has very, very different standards to me. If I go to her house and sit down on her sofa, when I get up to go to the loo she'll have puffed up my cushions before I get back. I never feel comfortable at her house. If she comes to mine, she'll plump up my cushions before she sits down. I'm not about to adapt to her way of doing things and she knows that now. When she comes to me, she has to live by my rules. There's an uneasy tension between us but we've come to a level of respect for one another."

"When I got married MIL gave me a trousseau of all the things I didn't have that I ought to have as a good wife – like napkins and paper table cloths. I never use them but it does make me feel guilty whenever I find them in the drawer; like I am falling below standard."

"We are from very different backgrounds – they did irritate me initially with the pettiness of their conversations. Before they met me they were very much meat and two veg people who had never had an Indian takeaway. MIL would say to me 'oh, I love what you've done with the salad' and I'd show her how to dress it with oil and vinegar she said 'I never have those things at home'. I think I completely opened their world."

"My MIL never eats out and always packs picnics when we go anywhere. I grew up in America where nearly every meal is out but I'm now falling into her way of doing things."

"My MIL used to dress like a flowery pair of curtains, everything was so dated. I said 'let's go shopping' and took her to some little boutiques. You should have seen her husband's face! Now she asks my opinion all the time and dresses really smartly. **"**

Wearing the trousers –
who's in charge?

"Power does not corrupt. Fear corrupts... perhaps the fear of a loss of power."

JOHN STEINBECK, THE SHORT REIGN OF PIPPIN IV (1957)

Power struggle seems to be at the root of many MIL-DIL relationship problems. Some daughter-in-laws experience, in their mother-in-law's presence, an overwhelming loss of control. Out of regard for MIL's seniority, her position as matriarch and years of experience, a softer DIL might step down and let MIL walk all over her.

This can be in matters as trivial as deciding what to have for dinner, or which bedtime story to read to the baby – in isolation, hardly worth getting upset about but over time, the obvious imbalance may wear away at DIL's self-esteem.

When DIL hands over absolute power in this way, willingly or otherwise, she may be prone to difficult, perhaps resentful, feelings, which can cause problems in the relationship. If DIL is built to please then keeping hold of the reins is easier said than done. A line in the sand is what is needed; DIL must state her case and stick to it.

MIL's dominion can make DIL feel silly and foolish and even exhibit immature behaviours. She is allowing herself to be treated like a child, rather than an equal.

It is likely that MIL will be oblivious to all of this. In her eyes, it is DIL who holds all the cards. DIL is the key to communication with MIL's son (often it is the DIL who prompts him to call) and access to grandchildren. DIL is keeper of the family calendar; nothing is arranged without her blessing and she will often give priority to her own parents, in terms of invites to school concerts and sports days.

One of the DILs I spoke to was a dentist who would never allowed her children to eat sugary sweets. She asked her MIL time and again to stop giving them to the grandchildren and eventually lost her patience and *banned* MIL from seeing the children for a whole month to 'teach her a lesson'.

This fear or suspicion – that DIL will steal away MIL's family – must lurk somewhere, beneath the ebb and flow of everyday relations. Is it a wonder that some MILs respond by tightening their grip?

She did not bring her beloved son into the world and lavish twenty to thirty odd years of time, money and effort over – only to hand him to DIL, on a plate, for her to toss about like a new plaything, to worry with petty gripes and complaints.

DIL must understand this unconscious need to influence the new domestic order. There may be comparable situations at work – perhaps think of MIL as a deposed line manager and you as the peppy new recruit, brought in over her head to do her old job; her experience is worth listening to but you must not let her bully you into submission.

DIL will have to show that she respects MIL's suggestions and interventions whilst, somehow, remaining in charge.

It is a tough call that most likely comes down to rhetoric – it's a good idea to intimate that husband is on your side – to remind MIL that you are a united (and grown-up!) front:

"Thank you so much for your suggestion but *we've* decided…"

"It's alright; *we've* got it sorted, thank you."

***

These comments are from DILs who say they find themselves feeling on the back foot in their MIL's presence. They illustrate perfectly, this shifting balance of power and loss of control:

" It's almost as though the energy changes whenever MIL steps over our doorstep. I am immediately on edge. I feel all knotted and anxious. I'll be tidying right until she comes through the door. She's no sooner in than she's issuing instructions or barking at my husband to move things around or put things up. The noise level goes right up. It's an air change – it's like we're in a whole different atmosphere all of a sudden. It's an incredible relief when I hear her car pull away. It's like my whole body relaxes. Sometimes it takes a few days to get over it."

"Whenever we're staying with the in-laws, if I speak to my mum, she always says I sound different – that my voice is strained, or that I'm 'not myself'. I guess she knows me best so she can tell how I'm feeling. I don't know why I'm just not able to relax there. It's like I'm afraid if I do let go, they won't like what they find. I suppose we're just different people."

"Very often, right after waving goodbye to MIL, I will immediately wipe down all the surfaces in my home. It is ridiculous, obsessive behaviour that doesn't reflect at all well on me. I am sure it has a lot to do with regaining control. I need to reassert myself – to put myself back in charge, as the woman of the house. It's primeval psychology, really. I feel like I'm beating my chest here. **"**

Teen Dad

Does your husband turn back into his teenage self when his mum comes to stay? Mine certainly does.

I won't see him for dust; it's as though he has a quiet word with himself: "*Two women in the house? No thanks, I'm off*", or, when bath-time is looming: "*the women have got it covered*," and with that, slopes off to some remote corner of the house, iPad in hand, leaving me to cope with the children *and* his mother. To him, having his mother visit signals a blissful, uninterrupted period of nag-free gaming.

I think it is quite common for couples not to speak to one another for the entire time that MIL is in the house. This is not MIL's fault – most MILs do not actively seek to drive a wedge between husband and wife – but it is often the effect of her presence. When there are any other grown-ups in the house, the men make hay (by themselves), just because they can.

They also tend to keep their heads well below the parapet if ever things do flare up between their wives and mothers. Obviously, they feel caught between two stools but there are times we wives would appreciate some backup. We get it that it's not their favourite subject, since it involves 'feelings', which generally sees them staring at their boots, wishing they were blessed with invisibility. They scratch their shiny pates and blink like Penfold from *Dangermouse*, muttering "Ooh-eck!" We understand they are embarrassed and uncomfortable, but there must be something they can do to help?

Mine seems to have a knack of saying precisely the wrong thing, at the wrong moment, primed to confirm his mother's worst fears about me and have me squirming in my seat; this might be spilling the beans about a drunken antic (largely past history now), exposing a white lie, or forcing me to admit that I haven't acted on MIL's advice. I want to kill him but have to laugh it off. I am super-mad at him for feigning obliviousness. Surely he must know how she will take all this? Does he not know his own mother? He seems to derive devilish pleasure from such trouble-making.

In my experience, husbands relieve themselves of all duty to communicate at the altar, right after saying "I do". It is usually the wives who have to remind them to call their parents. The men might tap in the numbers, if prompted, but will pass the phone over as quickly as they can, to 'her indoors', declaiming: "She knows more about this sort of stuff than me."

The sad truth is that lots of them are lazy ingrates who would go for months on end without picking up the phone to the poor woman who raised them.

A 'good' DIL will recognise that their husband's mother deserves more than that and will help keep MIL in the loop. It seems very unfair that DIL then gets the blame when MIL hasn't heard from you all in a while.

In the early days, whenever my husband did Skype a family member, he would invariably dial them up and then immediately go 'off task'; browse on a different screen, fiddle with the remote, or walk out of the room, abandoning me to the conversation.

I am much less daunted by this now that I have got to know them all much better, but I remember that back then, I wanted to kill him. The pressure of the video camera was too much for a postnatal mother to bear; I was often spilling out of a sexless nightie by 7pm and imagined them commenting on how I had let myself go!

At least he is not like those men who ring their mothers when they are down in the dumps and moan about their wives. This is BAD BAD news for you if you happen to be married to one of these. He must be stopped immediately. Poor MIL doesn't get your life in balance, she only hears the sharp end when he's feeling a bit miffed and inclined to offload but she won't understand that. All she will hear is "bad wife, unhappy son" – and it will keep her awake for nights on end. He needs to grow up and deal with his grievances himself, rather than go running to his mum.

On the domestic front, if your husband is about as useful as a chocolate teapot, it is tempting to blame his mother. I do sometimes gnash my teeth that mine didn't come to me fully house-trained.

I shouldn't grumble. After all, I found him under a tangle of wires, fluff and torn-up envelopes. We know what we are taking on. We cannot blame MIL when husbands fail to morph into the domestic dads of our dreams.

***

66 The first holiday I ever went on with my husband, before we were married, his mum had washed and packed all of his clothes and made him a food hamper. He was her little boy. Any problem he ever had, she would lift him out of it; that was why he always buried his head in the sand."

"My MIL always treats my husband like a little boy. She'll even call him 'little chappie', which he hates."

"My husband knows exactly how to play his mum. They have this little Frank Spencer routine they do. He'll turn it on for her when he gets in the door and she'll dissolve into giggles. He's literally playing her. It's gross, almost like flirting and I am completely excluded and she knows it."

"I was once chatting to MIL about men and how they never do anything around the house. I said I would never bring my sons up like that – then I remembered who I was talking to!"

"The quickest way for me to get my own way is to tell my MIL – my husband worships her."

"I don't think my husband has ever defended me against his mother. He never sees it as a direct attack. She is always extremely triumphant over me. Once, when she'd got my husband to take her out and I asked if they'd be back for dinner, she turned to me and said: 'you'll see us when you'll see us'. She glories in her power and gloats about it. To her it is a simple case of winning or losing."

"My husband finds it quite difficult to stand up to his parents for me because they are so controlling. They still treat him like a child."

"My MIL will ring up and say 'where's my son? I want my son.' She is always so rude to him. He's had to develop an asbestos hide. He just switches off when she's around. It's the only way he can deal with her but it means he will never stand up for me either."

"To be fair to my husband, he does back me up when it matters. Like the time I wanted to prove to MIL that giving tea too early could be dangerous to babies. She laughed at me so he looked it up on the internet, printed it out and took it round there as evidence."

"I always listen in on the upstairs phone when MIL rings up, just to make sure that she doesn't say anything bad about me! **99**

Some things are better left unsaid

"Sometime the truth hurts, and sometimes it feels real good."

HENRY ROLLINS, AMERICAN ROCK SINGER

Q: Is it always better to talk things through with your mother-in-law, or are there some situations where you should keep it to yourself?

"Don't be afraid of silence." One of my friends actually said this to her MIL, having struggled to hear her favourite TV show over the incessant chatter emanating from the sofa opposite.

Apparently, the poor lady burst into tears, necessitating a big old chat and make-up, so my friend missed her show anyway.

Perhaps this microcosmic flare-up could be interpreted as a warning to the rest of us: Some things are better left unsaid.

Remember that once spoken, you cannot take the words back. You might feel impassioned, hormonal, whatever, in the heat of the moment and determined to speak nothing but truth, to let MIL have it, right from the heart – but that might be very foolish indeed.

We are all taught to speak the truth. But when it comes to feelings, who is to say whether what you are currently experiencing is 'real'; in the sense of having an objectively identifiable cause? When you strip it back to the source, then MIL might not be at fault at all – the cause might be altogether imaginary and the feeling, only very fleeting – and yet you would take aim and shoot her right between the eyes.

Your 'truth', such as you see it, might be very damaging and cause a massive setback in the relationship from which you may never recover. Think carefully, if you should ever find yourself in this impulsive, emotional, confessional state of mind; the conversation you are about to have will always be there, forever, in the texture of your relationship.

It can throw you both so much off-kilter; you may not have the tools to repair the damage.

I have stood on this precipice myself – brimming with hormones dark and ruinous – and blundered over the edge, leaving all sense and reason behind. If I had wanted MIL's attention a few minutes earlier, now I had it, and I certainly didn't want it anymore. I tried to open my mouth, to excuse myself and all that came out was a strangled bleat.

How was I to explain myself? Even if she understood any of it, what possible solution might there be to such feelings? We are both stuck with who we are.

We all think we can smooth out relationships by talking things through. I would submit that that is not always the case. You can shoot yourself in the foot and open a can of worms (sometimes, only clichés will do) all at the same time. Once you take that lid off, there is no going back.

Far from making things easier between the two of you the situation is hyper-sensitised and it may be difficult for you to behave naturally towards one another, for quite some time.

It is hard enough to deal with negative voices in your own head, without inflicting them upon your poor mother-in-law as well.

Hence: some things are better unsaid.

66 I definitely this is a case where it's best not to show your workings. Do all your thinking and agonising in private and keep a brave face on it. There's no need to drag them down with you. Just so long as they think things are going well, that's the best you can hope for."

"I absolutely believe in the power of communication. If you all get round a table and thrash things out, you will get along fine. If you don't it turns into this horrible bubble and festers."

"I'm not sure that speaking your mind is a good thing. My mother-and-law and I get on only because I know when to shut up and bite my lip. She once wound me up so much, picking up my son, I knew I was about to lose it, so I just shut the door in her face instead. When I rang up later and apologised for having been so abrupt we just carried on as though nothing had happened. If I had let her have a piece of my mind, it would have taken us forever to get over it as she doesn't 'do' conflict.

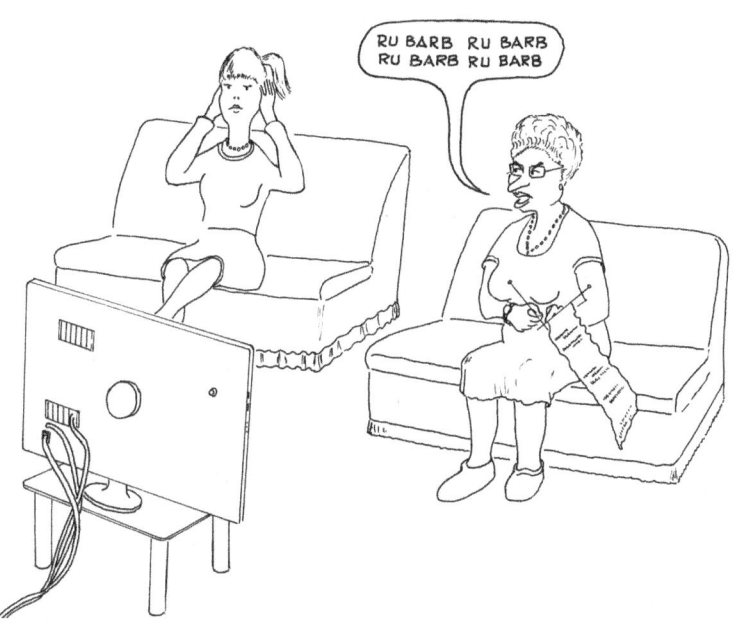

Keep your enemies close?

Is it better to have MIL living just around the corner or far, far away?

"My MIL is great, she's 1500 miles away." (Helen, 53)

Distance is no guarantee of a good relationship; I know of one mother-in-law who gave her DIL a nervous breakdown from the other side of the planet. The poor girl in question was already very fragile and the constant hectoring, by email and satellite link-up with her MIL in Australia destroyed what remained of her self-esteem. Skype has a lot to answer for!

Opinions are generally divided on this subject. Some women said they preferred to have MIL close by, not merely for convenience but because they could not imagine living under the same roof, even for the odd night.

Let us weigh up the pros and cons...

Round the corner:

MIL might pop in for a quick cup of tea, catch up on the latest news, help you fold a bit of washing, pick the children up from school and, most importantly, leave before bedtime. She might also babysit at the drop of a hat or have the children over to tea whilst you go for your fish pedicure. Sounds good so far...

...but then she also calls round unexpectedly whilst you're still lounging naked in bed and the kids are running riot, or step in the puddle of vomit in the driveway where you had a bit of trouble getting out of the taxi after PTA drinks the night before. She lets herself in with your spare key and reads your bank statements and whatever else is lying around on your desk, including your weekly calendar – so she can correct you if you claim that you are too busy to meet up. You are also at risk of setting precedents (having her for Sunday roast *every* week, or squeezing in a visit between Sainsbury's shop and the school pickup on Thursdays). Also remember that she is getting older – it won't be long before you're doing her shopping as well.

Far, far away...

MIL arrives with several suitcases that you have to lug up to the top of the house. She will sniff the linen to make sure she isn't being tucked into other grandma's sheets. She will then install herself at the kitchen table with her latest copy of *Good Housekeeping* and expect the first of many, many cups of tea. She'll still be there five days later, giving a running commentary on the minute by minute running of your household: "You don't iron your tea towels?"

She is the female incarnation of Harry Enfield's Mr *You-Don't-Wanna-Do-It-Like-That*; her visits are so rare, she is anxious to impart as much wisdom as possible on each occasion, to fix all those things you are doing wrong and shore up her own position as the one, true matriarch...

...on the other hand, she arrives with lovely, thoughtful presents for the children and bags full of shopping to restock your cupboards. She goes out of her way to spend quality time with the grandchildren, as she's anxious to make a lasting impression; she takes them out to beaches and castles and gets down on her hands and knees to play Hungry Hippos. She doesn't complain when they head upstairs at 6am and bounce up and down on her boobs and she always gets up and makes her special 'granny porridge'. She'll even sometimes bring you tea and toast in bed.

But don't take it from me. Let's hear it from some DILs...

Far away...

66   I think my kids know my in-laws better than my parents
        as they come and stay with us. It's about that quality of

stay. My own parents just pop in for a cup of tea but they don't get that special time."

"I think I would much prefer having a local MIL who can pop in and out, rather than someone who lands upon you, interrupting the continuous running of your household for a whole week or more. I know now that I can only cope with a restricted period of three days. Any more than that and we get this very strained build-up of tension. You can all be quite upbeat for three days. Any longer than that and it starts to make us all miserable. **99**

Down the road...

66 It's so much better that she's down the road. I wouldn't like to have them staying. I would feel like I had to be on my best behaviour. She'd keep me on my toes all the time. I know I can ring her if I'm going to be late from work and ask her to pick up the children for me."

"I'm just glad we never have to have everyone to stay for Christmas. I honestly believe we'd kill each other."

"I like being able to visit and leave when we want to. Fortunately, my in-laws are quite old-fashioned, they don't arrive uninvited. We always make an arrangement. I think I would struggle to keep my mouth shut if they were actually staying here for any length of time. **99**

In a granny annex...

66 My MIL lives with us, in the other half of the house. We are separated by a lockable door, which I think is very important. It does have its good and bad points. It's great for babysitting and she'll do my ironing and gardening but she'll also let herself in when we're not there and tidy up. I know she's been in when all my sofa cushions have been straightened. There's also the expectation that we'll have her every Sunday for lunch. She'll say, 'oh, no dear I won't come in' – but then she always does!

"She also likes to potter about in our garden – when the boys kicked a football into the flowerbeds she said 'oh, no boys, not at my petunias' and I thought, hmm, don't you mean *my* petunias?"

"It is difficult all living together. Because we are really living in her house, it does feel like we have sold our souls to the devil. I know she still looks at us sometimes and thinks 'not in my house'. She does plan to move out, eventually and I'm hoping she'll put all her energies into her new home and building a new life – but somehow I doubt it. I'm worried she'll never be able to leave us in peace.

"

On the farm...

" There's no privacy in farming families. I don't know anyone else who sees their MIL every day of their lives. You really are marrying your husband's parents as well. In the beginning, MIL she was in our house all the time – if I had friends for the weekend she would come in as though she still lived there. It was very awkward to have to chat to my mates with her hovering over the kettle. Things couldn't go on like that. It just didn't feel like our home. I had a few days where I ended up in tears.
I knew I would have to be grown up about it otherwise we were going to end up screaming at one another. We all had to work out where we were and establish our boundaries very carefully.
She had to see that she would retain her place as matriarch and that I wasn't going to take over. She had always done the teas for everyone dropping into the farmhouse – I reassured her that I wasn't going to take over, or do her job. I didn't want to be tipping grain or lambing sheep as I had my own business.

"Things are so much better now. I think she sees how hard
I work for the family and she respects that. Now MIL
looks in my cupboards and sees they're bare and goes
off shopping for me, which I love. I value her support
tremendously and could not survive without it. We talk to
each other about everything.
I'll ask her advice about cutting my roses and she'll come
to me for fashion tips. She sews on all my name tapes for
me and does my book-keeping. She'll even see if I buy a
pair of knickers online. Sure, there are some days when
I'll close the door and have a wobble but I think it is a
great testament to how well we've learned to manage the
relationship that we have only ever fallen out twice in
almost a decade.   **99**

Big family holidays

Holidays can cause so much trouble.

You want to go to your mum's for Christmas because all the cousins will be there and you know you will all have much more fun – but you went to your mum's last year as well. Grandma – the other one – is going to flip.

Be careful not to set a precedent, especially with regards to important holidays – of going to one family then another. It will be tricky to break the cycle without causing offence.

The smart thing to do is to get in early and state your plans. Then everybody knows what they are dealing with. Also, there is nothing wrong with staying at home, if you can handle the cooking...

I remember one year deciding we were much too grown up to throw ourselves on grandparent hospitality and that we really we should be doing Christmas for ourselves now. I had one eye on *Delia's Christmas* and the other on Tesco online, I was only two paragraphs in to 'Traditional Roast Turkey with Pork Sage and Onion Stuffing' when I picked up the phone.

"I know we said we weren't coming, but how big, exactly, is your turkey?"

My mother-in-law is a magnificent cook. I was a hapless rookie. I just couldn't do it to my family.

As your children grow up and the older generation gets more tired and less enthusiastic about hosting, MIL might be delighted to be invited to you, for a change. Or you might announce that you are having a quiet family Christmas, but will visit everyone on Boxing Day. So long as you take parents' and in-laws' feelings into account, they have little cause to feel aggrieved.

Remember, Christmas is only fun for children. For grown-ups it is often uncomfortable, exhausting and ultimately disappointing. Don't blame MIL. Blame Santa for giving you unrealistic expectations. Family wars at Christmas are inevitable; there are entire websites devoted to avoiding conflict on the big day – you are lucky if you escape without a stabbing.

Regarding holidays away, mums of small children are much more inclined to invite parents and in-laws along, especially in the early days, to embrace the benefits of in-house babysitting. Spending a week cooped up in a cottage with MIL may be very different from sharing the odd cup of tea and gossip about the grandchildren. Go in with your eyes open.

***

66 Steve's parents have paid to take us all away quite a few times but we have to do everything together. We eat together; go on days out together etc. We got with Steve's sister as well but they are so different to us and like to stay in bed until lunchtime. We end up looking after their kids as well as ours. Steve's parents are so desperate for everyone to get on it puts us all under pressure and no one can relax and be themselves. They've suggested we all go away again next year and I feel like we can't say no, or they'll think we are ungrateful, or didn't enjoy ourselves last time."

"We have hardly any time off during the year and it annoys me that there is this expectation that we will all go on a big family holiday together. Our family time is so precious we want to be together without anyone else. I've suggested my husband go and see them by himself with the children."

"If we go on holiday with my parents my husband's parents get very jealous. Everything we do with one, we feel we have to 'pay back' the other."

"We went on a family holiday with my in-laws. There was an arrangement we would all take turn cooking. I was quite heavily pregnant and our little girl had been up all night vomiting, but no-one offered to help. We were slaving away in the kitchen and having to run up and down the stairs checking on our kids and everyone else was out on the patio getting pissed. I didn't say anything but I was quietly furious."

"My in-laws are very jealous that we spend so much time with my family in Germany. They think I am dragging their son and grandchildren over there. They don't appreciate that actually my husband loves the lifestyle over there. My kids really know my parents – my dad takes them for walks and sailing and rowing on the lakes. My in-laws never put themselves out or do anything with us. Is it surprising that we all prefer to go to Germany?"

"We always used to go to the in-laws on Boxing Day until we got married. Then I said that whoever wanted to come to us could come, but that we were staying put for Christmas. You can't be yourselves in someone else's house. I didn't want to have to walk on eggshells and censor myself anymore."

"We were trying to plan a holiday in a cottage in the Lakes with the whole family. My sister-in-law said: 'well, seeing as Jane can't really take the baby, she could have the children and we'll all go for walks'. I could see how that one was going to work out and I wasn't going to have it. **99**

Pancakes

Sometimes, we DILs just have to admit when we are beat.

In my case, it is in the kitchen. I'm doing a lot better these days but I know I will never match up to the culinary prowess of my mother-in-law.

MIL is the archetypal domestic goddess. She is Madame Merigot, Julia Child, Alice Waters and Nigella reconfigured in the personage of one very English, very sensible, eminently capable cook. I can scarcely boil an egg. This is shameless hyperbole but you get the point. MIL musters up feasts fit for a king with octopi-an dexterity; whipping with one hand, frying with another, peeling onions with her teeth. Before the morning is out, she will have produced three tarts (one savoury, two sweet), four vegetable dishes (never simply boiled), a gorgeous glazed baked ham and Cumberland sauce and a large jug of real custard. All to die for.

The kitchen, however, in the wake of this onslaught looks as though it has borne the brunt of a force 12 hurricane. Think *The Wreck of the Hesperus* with added detritus. The phrase 'you can't make an omelette without breaking eggs' only goes so far. I am not sure it explains the annihilation of domestic order that follows a MIL cooking storm. It is as though she has stood in the centre of the room with a five pound bag of flour, whirling it above her head, smearing butter all over her work surfaces and flicking sauce up the walls. Nothing is safe. One taste of her creations though and you'll believe it's worth the washing up.

Needless to say, MIL makes the most excellent pancakes.

This is her failsafe pancake recipe, as she emailed to me. Follow it exactly and you will be a kitchen hero.

5ozs water	5ozs plain flour
5ozs milk	2 1/2 ozs melted butter
2 egg yolks	1 tablespoonful sugar
1 whole egg	pinch of salt

Three tablespoons orange liqueur (Grand Marnier, Cointreau or other) you can substitute rum or brandy.

Place all in a blender or Cuisinart and blend. Wait 30 minutes or more. Blend again and pour into a jug. Thin if necessary, with milk to consistency of thin cream.

Have warm plates, warmed maple syrup, halved juicy lemons and good jersey cream.

You need a small ladle and a flat crepe pan (or frying pan). Over a HIGH HEAT, get the thick bottomed pan VERY hot – this is the key. Add a 1/2 flat teaspoon of butter - it should sizzle and brown quickly.

Pour in a small ladleful of mixture and tip and swill to cover the bottom of the pan in a very thin layer. It should rapidly set and brown at the edges. Loosen edges with a spatula and slide it under the crepe – loosen it and flip it over.

After another couple of minutes reverse the pan over a plate and let the pancake fall into the centre of it (the first one often spoils). Repeat until all the mixture is used up and you have a pile of crepes.

To serve, put a crepe flat on a warm plate and pour a little maple syrup on it and quickly fold into four. Repeat so that each person has three or four. Pour more syrup over and a little cream and plenty of squeezed lemon juice.

**

Unfortunately, last year, I received her recipe too late. I already had a spectacular pancake failure on my hands by the time I opened her email.

This was my reply :

Alternatively, take one packet of pancake ready mix.

Add too much milk.

Pour excessive olive oil into frying pan.

Add too much batter.

Swill it round too slowly leaving large holes.

Panic.

(Pancakes are in imminent danger due to excess oil.)

Tip oil down the sink knowing you really shouldn't.

Settle pan back on stove confident all will be well now.

Worry.

Pancakes appear to be burning yet stuck fast.

Attempt to slide palette knife under pancake.

Pancake will fall to pieces.

Don't be too hard on yourself. This was doomed from the start.

Scrape the whole mess on to plastic plate, sprinkle with sugar and offer to the German tenant, who knows no better.

BUT MUMMY YOU SAID YOU DID'NT
WANT GRANDMA TO COME TODAY !!

Gag your monsters

How is it that children know precisely what to say, at the very worst of moments, to get you into the steamiest heap of trouble?

Perhaps their social awareness is more finely tuned than we give them credit for at aged two or three. When they look up at granny, all wide-eyed and innocent and remark, "Mummy said she didn't want you to come today", isn't there just the faintest hint of a smirk on their lips?

Obviously, I'm not the only one whose children drop them right in it.

***

66 They'll say to me, in front of her, 'so mummy, what do you *really* think of gransie?' I will go to pieces, thinking, *where the bloody hell did that just come from?"*

"My in-laws always take my kids to McDonald's. They think they are giving them a treat as I won't allow it. One time, as they were picking the kids up, my eldest says to them: "My mummy says that McDonald's is for lazy people who can't cook."

"There is definitely competition about which grandparent gets to see us more and grandma is particularly sensitive about it. For some reason, my children have decided to switch what they call them, always calling her 'granny' instead. The more I try and squash it, the more they do it."

"My mother-in-law is very sensitive about her age. Harry has got a thing about grabbing her jowls and saying: 'grandma, what's that bit there? Or, he'll sit on her lap and grab one of her rolls and say 'grandma, what's that under your top?' That's when I'll jump in and say 'would you like another cup of tea, grandma?'"

"My daughter asked MIL why she wore a nightie in bed, adding: 'My mummy never wears anything in bed'."

"Once, my MIL came down to breakfast still in her nightie and it made her look enormous. I knew what Sam was going to say, even before he said it, but there was nothing I could do. He came right out with it: 'granny, why are you so fat?' She was very good about it and said: 'because I eat too much'."

"We only see the in-laws a couple of times a year, at best; MIL likes the children to call her Nanna Anna. Once, MIL arrived before a card that she had sent and one of my children opened it right in front of her. They said: 'Nanna Anna? Who's she?' I was mortified."

99

Sometimes you drop yourself in it...

66 I was in hospital, having just given birth to my third child when my husband came in an announced 'mum's not happy'. He said she had been at home colouring with my little girl, on a big jumbo colouring pad, when she'd found a picture of a witch. Underneath it, I had written 'Granny Janet'. When he told me that my heart literally stopped and I think I burst into tears. Dan saw how upset I was and the panic in my face and told me he had just been winding me up (I had just had a baby, after all!) and that of course she didn't see it. About a month later he admitted that she had –he still had the crumpled picture in his jacket pocket where she'd ripped it out!"

"I used to write for a local magazine. One month I wrote all about how my MIL had been upset with us for buying a house in the middle of nowhere. It was quite cathartic – I didn't hold back - and I thought she would never in a million years see it as they lived a long way away. Then, by chance, they happened to visit the same week it came out. We were having lunch in a pub and I saw her eyes rest upon a copy of the magazine. I wanted to leap in and snatch it away but it was too late, she went right to it, saying 'isn't this the magazine you write for, Lizzie?' I watched her face as she read it through. I couldn't even remember what I had written but she kept saying 'oh my' and 'oh!' getting louder and louder. I made some excuse about it being all poetic licence."

"We were in the hospital visiting my mother-in-law, who used to work as a nurse herself. My daughter and I were sitting by her bed, chatting to one of the nurses:
'So what do you want to be when you grow up?' the nurse asked.
'A doctor!' Hannah replied.
'Oh, not a nurse then?'
'Nah', said Hannah, 'mummy says they're not very bright'. 99

Cultural differences

One the one hand, a language barrier might be just the ticket when dealing with mother-in-law.

If you disagree with something she is saying, you can shrug your shoulders and shake your head, pretending that the conversation has gone beyond your humble grasp of the language.

Aside from that not inconsiderable advantage, however, surely it is even more difficult getting on with a woman who lives thousands of miles away (or could this be a blessing?), is the product of an alien culture, adhering to odd traditions and who quite possibly blames you for dragging her beloved son away from her, to live out his days in a foreign country?

I know of one Italian consultant surgeon in his late 40s, whose own mother still Skypes or telephones him from Tuscany, three times every day – even at his work, for updates. I dread to think what this woman does to his wife.

***

South American MIL (Claire's story)

66 The language barrier can be both a help and a hindrance; it's a help because you can't have any sort of in-depth conversation which might reveal your differences. But I found it very difficult when it came to explaining:

that you'd like to have a natural birth on all fours (with a doula) according to your hypno-birthing training and;

your reasons for this, especially if that is not how things are done in her country.

There, births tend to be extremely medicalised with a huge emphasis on intervention, so it was a real challenge to explain to her that yes, I did expect the 'eminent doctor' to get down on the floor and actually catch the baby!

It can be difficult to resolve a situation when people are approaching it from trenchantly opposed cultural positions. MIL will have been doing certain things in a certain way for years, just as her mother did before her and so on. So when you, as a new mum, approach things in a seemingly foreign way, there is certainly room for conflict.

99

Breast vs Formula

66 With us, the battleground was the *breast vs formula* debate. Formula is possibly the more favoured approach in my MIL's country, and she would make statements such as "when you can't produce enough milk" or "you might find your milk is too rich for the baby". I was determined to breastfeed but knew that if I found it a challenge, I wouldn't have much support at home.

Once, when my baby was crying a lot in the middle of the night, MIL came into the bedroom brandishing a bottle of formula and of course my husband was on her side. She had brought up all of his brothers and sisters, after all, and they grew up to be healthy and happy human beings, so how could she be wrong?

This tipped me over the edge (fragile new mum that I was) and I moved out with the baby to stay with my parents who were visiting for a couple of weeks. It caused a temporary rift, but it didn't last long - I knew she only wanted the best for the baby and to help us get some sleep.

99

Sugary treats

66 The other thing that worried me was MIL's attitude
to sugar and sweets. Over there they don't seem at all
concerned by the quantities of sugar and additives in sweets
and drinks, so are very happy to give babies sweets to suck
and sugary squash to drink etc. I was horrified to learn that
MIL also put sugar in her grandchildren's formula. I tried
to make my feelings very clear to my husband, so it would
subtly filter through to MIL but I think he thought I was
making a fuss about nothing. Apparently, she came back
with: "how am I supposed to treat your children if I can't
give them sweets and nice drinks?"

We also disagreed about the temperature of the
apartment. I would quietly turn the temperature of the air
conditioning unit down - it was about 38 degrees outside,
and I thought 20C inside was fine for me and the baby -
but for her that was freezing. I'm sure she thought I was out
of my mind and endangering his health, so would not so
subtly turn it back up again to about 26C.

Generally, however, MIL seems to be more amused (or
occasionally bemused) by any cultural differences we might
have, rather than critical about them. Once I became quite
fluent, we found that we got on very well, luckily! 99

**

66 My in-laws are southern Europeans. They liked to go out
for dinner after 8pm as a family and couldn't understand
why we wouldn't take the kids. My children are in bed
by 7pm. I'm quite strict on routine like that. Now they're
older and I've relaxed a bit more, we get on better."

"I always go out running whenever we go over to see the
in-laws in Spain. Daily. It deals with the stress hormones,
gets rid of all the calories (from comfort eating and

drinking your way through the trip) and you get an hour of meditative alone time. Plus you get to explore the local countryside. It's foolproof!"

"My MIL is an English emigrant, so language is not an issue. However, she has adopted French ways with great enthusiasm and denigrates all things English at every opportunity. Particular friction arises when she undermines English mythological traditions such as the Easter bunny, Father Christmas and the tooth fairy. It's hard to maintain a lie when someone is insisting in front of your kids that their lie is better!"

"I think you can be blunter as a non-native speaker, which often comes across as quite brutal. I'm from Poland and am not that subtle. I am very direct and I think my English in-laws do sometimes find me quite frightening and possibly also rude. **99**

Working DILs

There is no argument, as far as many mothers-in-law are concerned; the grandchildren must come first and that's that. DIL's ambitions have to take a back seat, or we are condemned as unnatural and selfish mothers.

I remember my mum saying, when my eldest was only a few months old, "Well, life moves on - it's his turn now", as though my own aspirations had gone up in smoke with the placenta.

I might have misunderstood her meaning (especially as she herself worked right through our childhood) but, fragile new mum that I was, I bristled.

Chances are that we DILs expect more from life. We were brought up to believe that we had an equal shot at a decent career as the boys. It comes as a bit of a surprise when, all of a sudden, the brakes are applied.

Some mums – particularly those who have been breaking their necks working all hours of day and night in fiendishly demanding jobs – are relieved to catch the bus out of there, for a time at least. These women (who have an option to go back) are easy to spot – they are generally chirpier and more grateful for their time at home than those with no promise of 'escape'. These other poor darlings may be identified by their thousand-yard stare as they look through you, towards the event horizon.

Of course, not everyone has the luxury of choice. The most common reason for returning to work nowadays is financial necessity (68% according to the most recent NCT survey); to put food on the table and pay the mortgage.

It's a little trickier to find our moral compass when the decision is a question of financial improvement – to be able to enjoy nice holidays and a newer car, for example – as squared with the children's happiness and security.

And harder still, if the only reason for mum to go back to work is for intellectual stimulation: to boost her self-esteem and pander to her ego . In MIL's day, a working mother was a rarity. Nowadays, the stay-at-home mum is fast becoming a figure of ridicule; government incentives, such as childcare vouchers for families with two working parents have been criticised for 'stigmatising' mothers who stay at home to care for their children.

The decision is far from straightforward, with so many factors – cultural, personal and financial – weighing upon it. Things might have been very different for MIL. Life has leaped forward since the 1960s and 70s.

It is not very fair of MIL to print out the latest *Femail* article on separation anxiety and mental health problems in adult life on grandchild's first full day at nursery; or from that moment on, to refer to him only as 'poor Mikey'.

But neither is it entirely reasonable of us to expect her to say nothing at all (especially if we are leaning on her to fill in our childcare gaps). She believes very firmly that full-time day care is no substitute for a mother's love; that there is nothing more important than raising the next generation; that the only recipe for a confident, self-assured adult is an available mother. It would be wise of her to do her nail-biting in private and to tone it down with you, but as the children's grandmother, she must be entitled to have an opinion. You will need to be able to listen, without taking offence, and have the courage of your convictions, whatever they may be.

***

A lot of MILs find it hard to watch how our generation are doing things. Most women work now. It's a normal part of family life."

"I know my MIL thinks I shouldn't work full-time. She didn't work for five years whilst her children were young and then only went back part-time. She's never said anything though. She's got more sense."

"My husband only worked for two days a week for three years. MIL was pretty shocked. She wouldn't ever have expected him to do that. That's something Matt's dad would never have done. For us as a couple, it was brilliant. It means Matt has experience of being the main carer. It was hard for me, though. I would be getting home just in time to give them a bath if I was lucky and they would say 'I want daddy, mummy go away'. I think now, in retrospect, my MIL sees that it was lovely for Matt to have been so involved."

"I am lucky in that my mother-in-law would never have presumed to judge me for going back to work. She was a sweet woman who was merely concerned that I was pushing myself too hard."

"I know that MIL felt uncomfortable that I had gone back full-time and worried about the impact on my children. She didn't need to say anything – I knew how she felt but I just had to ignore it. It's hard enough trying to balance and juggle everything without chewing yourself up about what your mother-in-law might think."

"I know that I need to work - to be fully engaged, or the bogeymen come to call. I crave the stimulation and recognition of the workplace – nobody claps you for doing the ironing. I have quite an embarrassing need to prove myself. I think it has a lot to do with my mum's example. She was an anomaly in her time. She managed to work full-time right through both babies without employing a nanny or putting my brother and me into full-time nurseries. She was a superwoman. She did it by breaking her back. By carting us round with her and taking us into the office; by dashing out in the middle of meetings to spoon gloopy lumps into grumpy mouths. Why did she do it? Because she was consumed with guilt that she was abandoning us and failing in her duties as a mother, trying to have it all."

"I wouldn't be able to go back to work if it wasn't for my MIL. She has been a fantastic support. She couldn't have done more to help."

"When I first went back to work, MIL was very pleased to help and said she'd have my daughter every Wednesday. Then, gradually, she would ring and say she felt ill, or had something important on and I realised I couldn't rely on her. I'm not sure it's fair to expect them to tie themselves down to such a regular commitment. Also, you feel you have to be so grateful about it. It's much better if you can sort things out yourselves."

"I think perhaps my MIL envies my work. She wasn't able to have a career. She found the whole child-rearing thing a nightmare and didn't really enjoy being stuck at home with a rotten baby. So she's partly cross with me for dumping her grandchildren in nursery and partly envious that she didn't have the same opportunity."

"Sometimes, I think MIL is frustrated that my job isn't better than it is. She thinks 'if you are going to dump the kids in childcare, at least make sure it is worth it'. 99

Family feuds and contact disputes

If you cannot find a way to get along with your mother-in-law, you may be heading for family breakdown. Perhaps you are even considering withdrawing contact with grandchildren. Do not underestimate the hurt that this will cause.

Lynn Chesterman, chief executive of the Grandparents' Association, told me: "Everyone seems to think family breakdowns are to do with divorce and separation, whereas in our experience it only accounts for 50%. The rest are caused by wider family feuds."

The association receives around 5,000 calls from grandparents every year, about contact disputes alone (where grandparents have been denied access to grandchildren). Of those, she estimates that nearly 2,000 are caused by 'personality clashes' between daughter-in-law and mother-in-law.

"The classic problem used to be between the husband and the wife's mother, now things appear to have switched and it's often the male partner's mother who can be quite difficult," she said.

Just as I thought. I had plenty of questions to ask…

Why are you seeing more feuding between MILs and DILs?

"I do think it is something to do with the temperature of our times; that people of all age groups are living increasingly more selfishly. The idea that we're doing x, y or z and everyone else has to bend to us. If everyone is doing that then things aren't going to go very well – society can't function.

"My personal view is that mothers and sons are often very close. I think that mums can often forget when they take a partner that the partner moves up to number one. You either accept that, or you don't. In some cases, the MIL will almost say 'it's me or her'.

"You might not get on, but you just have to learn to bite your tongue unless it's something that directly impacts on you. She is your son's choice. Surely it is right that he puts her first?"

When are grandparents deprived of contact with their grandchildren?

"We find that lack of contact with grandchildren tends to follow after things have really soured. We would say that if things are still going along alright, even if you do find it difficult, you really have to find a way to keep it to yourself. Have a shout in the corner, or in the shower but whilst the relationship is there (even if it is not to your liking, or if you can't stand the person) then do everything you can to keep it going, for the sake of the grandchildren. Prevention is better than cure.

"If it has got to the point where DIL has stopped all contact then (your own behaviour) must have impacted upon the son, as well, to some extent. Yes, he's in the middle and we hear grandparents say 'but he's weak, he won't stand up to her', but think about whether you might be being unrealistic.

"Can you meet halfway? Consider whether what you are asking might be a bit over the top. Some grandparents are upset that they are not allowed to see the children every Saturday. With the best will in the world, where both parents are working during the week, it is just not fair to expect them to enter into such a regular arrangement."

What can be done to resolve chronic problems?

"For heaven's sakes, don't threaten court action. In very extreme circumstances, that may be the way to go but try everything else first. We have a very good template letter on our website, which is quite powerful, even if you don't add anything more to it. It appeals to the daughter-in-law to let the grandparents see the grandchildren for their benefit.

"To cut off one side is not fair, especially if the children have seen them quite a lot. She is hurting the children, cutting off one side of their heritage. We see this particularly where the DIL has separated from her partner; don't start by criticising her new partner. That won't get you anywhere.

"If the grandchildren are happy at home and mum and dad or stepdad, are together, they can't be doing such a bad job. The grandparent needs to shift her attitude and be more accepting. Every generation has their different ways of doing things, different pressures upon them, different opportunities. It wasn't so long ago that the papers were all full of one parent families and latch key kids – now if the mum doesn't go out to work, she must be a benefit scrounger. They are under totally different pressures to the generations that have gone before."

So how should MILs and DILs keep things on the rails?

"For mothers-in-law, I think it is a good idea to ask themselves, when they got married, what sort of interference would they have liked? In my case, the answer was 'none' – so why should I do that to my daughter-in-law?

"The daughter-in-law should remember that MIL is a mum as well and has brought up her own children perfectly well – and not act as though her mother is the only one capable of looking after the grandchildren. Sometimes that can really hurt. She mustn't forget that both grannies have the same feelings towards the grandchildren. The number of times I have heard DILs saying 'my mum would *never* do that...' as though their own mother is perfect – I think hang, on, now, be fair.

"Also, the two families might have very different financial circumstances. One might be able to take you and the kids to Disney whilst the other can barely scratch a dinner together. Be equally grateful for their generosity.

"It's not too much to ask for you to sit with MIL for a couple of hours, nodding and smiling, no matter what you might feel inside – or, if you really can't take it, why don't you ask your partner if he can take the kids to his mum's for the afternoon whilst you go shopping or get your hair done?"

For more information visit www.grandparents-association.org.uk or contact the Grandparents' Association helpline on 0845 4349585.

Getting back on track

Can we pull back from a damaged relationship?

I have been dismayed at the number of DILs who have told me that communication has all but broken down between themselves and their in-laws – those DILs who say: "We don't see them if we can help it", or "I don't want anything more to do with her".

Presumably these families have tried to work things out between them; some have even been to family mediation, but the women in question – and quite possibly the in-laws too – feel they have come to the end of the line. In their own minds, they have tried everything and it is too hurtful to prolong the battle.

Are there really relationships that are completely irredeemable? These families have reached an impasse but surely there must be some way of pulling back from that point and setting off down a new track?

Samantha believes that all problems can be resolved with open and honest communication. She was wearing herself thin trying to be a 'proper' farmer's wife and manage her own HR business all at the same time, believing MIL would think badly of her if she parted from tradition. The strain of it caused her to resent her in-laws' help, which she interpreted as implicit criticism.

She believes it is up to DILs to recognize the need for a 'grown-up' conversation, to iron out any grievances in a dispassionate, clear-headed fashion.

66 It's about getting the measure of one another and knowing what you expect of one another. I used to feel I had to get up and put breakfast out for everyone – that it was

expected of me as the farmer's wife – now I just say there are the cupboards, bring your own rolls. I begrudged the fact that my in-laws were in our house every day, because of this underlying sensitivity, and now I absolutely don't. They have shown that they respect what I do. We talked it all through and have a much clearer division of roles now. **99**

If MIL and DIL are at loggerheads, then one of them will have to climb a few rungs down the ladder, or they will never broker peace. Of course, it could be that DIL does not want to make up – it might suit her to keep her mother-in-law at a distance. One lady admitted:

66 I haven't spoken to my MIL for six months, since she told me I was a bad mother for leaving my son at day nursery until 6pm. I can't help it, I have to work. It's actually been a relief to be able to feel that we can live our lives our way without worrying about her getting wound up about it all the time. **99**

Unless MIL has, deliberately and maliciously, wreaked real and lasting harm, however (try to be objective here), then I believe that DIL must do everything she can to sort things out. Inconvenience, dislike, frustration, annoyance, difference of opinion – none of these is sufficient cause to cut MIL off. We have to find it in our hearts to substitute these baser sentiments for kindness and tolerance.

MIL is still our husband's mother and a grandmother to our children (if we have any). The notion of duty may be outmoded, but we do have a responsibility to maintain some sort of relationship with her. We don't get to write her out altogether. It is not our decision to make.

Relationships fluctuate, through the years; circumstances change and we all grow a little older and (one hopes) wiser. It is not healthy to cling on to past disagreements. If things are bad, with more effort, they can be improved. If things are good, we mustn't get complacent. The relationship demands regular attention. Communicating with MIL might not come naturally; the quality of your relationship will likely be determined by how much effort you are prepared to put in.

By putting yourself out and factoring her in, unless she is a monster, you should be able to get things back on track.

66 My MIL and I didn't get on for three years. She hated my guts. She and I are very different. Her husband has been ill and I've been there helping day and night. Now she's decided she likes me. I would say you have to stick to your guns and not be battered down. Don't lose yourself belief and don't let them tip you off centre. They'll come round eventually."

"I think MIL has finally come to accept me. She now realises, after 12 years that she can't get rid of me. I'm not going anywhere and I have got three of her grandchildren. We do get along better now but I wouldn't completely trust her. She might revert back to how she was. I'm always conscious that she's been quite nasty to me in the past."

"I've given up trying now. I used to bend over backwards to be nice but it always backfired. I always managed to say the wrong thing. Like the time that I thought I'd research MIL's family name and managed to trace her ancestors back to Ireland. I thought she'd be delighted that I'd shown an interest. Ben was kicking me under the table all the time I was speaking. I said: 'I've traced it right back to the 1800s – did you know that you were part of the Irish Mac Lochlainns?' It all went quiet. Then she said: 'I hate the Irish'. We've never spoken of it again. Maybe she thought I was deliberately needling her. She's a very difficult woman."

"I know people say you have to keep trying for the sake of the kids but I'm not sure what they get out of it. She is so useless with them. I do think there comes a time when you have to put yourselves first as a family and decide you're not going to be hurt anymore."

"I once had a very pivotal phone call, in my relationship with my MIL. Before then, when she rang, she'd always bark at me: 'I want to speak to my son' and I'd hand him over. Then, one time, she rang back again, half an hour later and said: 'I think I might have been a bit abrupt to you, wasn't I Janet? I think I could have spoken to you, couldn't I Jan?' I said: 'Of course you could, Annie' and from that moment on, we had a relationship. But we were in our third decade of marriage before we got to that point."

"I think it is okay to reach a point where you recognise that you will only ever have a polite relationship, at a distance. My in-laws will drive all the way over from East Anglia to drop of Easter eggs, have a forty-five-minute cup of tea and then drive all the way back. I know that his mother has a big problem with me and it used to upset me dreadfully. I am not the woman she would have liked her son to marry. The kids do like being with them and they are good grandparents, so now we send them down there in the summer for three days at a time, without us. I used to think that it was up to me to put my feelings aside for the sake of the kids and my husband; to bite my lip and not cause problems. It was my mum who said to me, having seen how MIL speaks to me, that for my own sanity I had to remove myself. She said 'it's not healthy – they obviously don't like you'."

"I have noticed a real thaw in the last few years as she realises that we're going to have to help her out in her old age."

"As an older DIL, I would say that all the things that I've learned that could have made our relationship a bit better, I found out too late!"

"My MIL died quite recently. We were in a good place by the end, but it took us a very long time. It's like she hung on for the family's sake to heal its wounds. I like to think she's doing some magic up there."

"I think MILs tend to adopt a persona with their DILs. If you see them out with other people, their husbands or friends, they can be very different. That's a good thing in that it means they might be able to change the way they are with you."

"It could be the case that your in-laws feel they need an invitation to see you and yet you've assumed they know they have an open invitation to come at any time. Often, sorting things out will be a case of trying to see things from MIL's perspective."

"It might help to remember that we are all future MILs in waiting – perhaps we would be more sympathetic. **"**

Escape the stereotype

Fact of the day: *In British slang c.1884, mother-in-law was "a mixture of ales old and bitter"!*

There are certain terms that are commonly associated with mothers-in-law; certainly from DIL's perspective, that is. Look up MIL in the daughter-in-law dictionary and you might find the following entry:

Mother-in-law [muhth-er-in-law]

Noun, plural mothers-in-law

The mother of one's husband or wife

Origin: 1350-1400; Middle English *modyr in lawe*

Synonyms: over-bearing, interfering, controlling, demanding, intrusive, oppressive, insensitive…

MIL might retaliate with a few choice words of her own, for daughters-in-law: over-sensitive, manipulative, passive-aggressive, ungrateful, selfish, prickly, petty, lazy…"

We are talking lowest common denominator here, but these terms crop up, again and again, especially where relationships have veered off course.

Could it be that we carry around with us these stubborn stereotypes and expect MIL to play to form? Are we looking for these failings, even when there is little real evidence that they exist? Don't we, on some level, want to find MIL wanting, to confirm what we (albeit subconsciously) know to be true?

Our antennae are continuously on the alert for the slightest nuance that might suggest a possible infringement of our boundaries. Yes, we cry, she is interfering. She is behaving precisely as she should in these circumstances. All's right with the world.

This is likely a two-way thing: MIL will scrutinise us for evidence that we are 'controlling' her son, conspiring to have everything our way and overreacting when things go against us. Again, these judgements are often rooted in the scantiest of evidence; seek and ye shall find.

How many times have we heard MILs remark of their daughters-in-law: "Of course he always does what *she* says…" or, "no, I wouldn't dare! *She* wouldn't allow it."

What if we were all to try very hard to resist the pull of the stereotype and refuse to let preconceptions colour our judgement?

Then we might be able to escape from the roles that thousands of years of human civilisation has fashioned for us – that of the over-sensitive, 'difficult' DIL, or the interfering, overbearing MIL – and create whole new prototypes, the moderate, charitable, tolerant and reasonable DIL and the kind, considerate, thoughtful, respectful and understanding MIL.

It won't happen overnight and it takes more than a little self-discipline to override instinct and base nature but we are not savages – we are all capable of establishing civil, workable relationships if we graft at it.

Obviously, some MILs are more difficult than others, but a big-hearted DIL goes a very long way toward offsetting a tricky MIL.

Don't go looking for trouble.

Here is a stirring quotation from the American poet Ralph Waldo Emerson to inspire you to do better:

"Be not the slave of your own past – plunge into the sublime seas, dive deep, and swim far, so you shall come back with new self-respect, with new power, and with an advanced experience that shall explain and overlook the old."

Top tips for Managing MIL

Okay, so those of you looking for something of a quick fix may have skipped straight to this section. So try these for size – 15 ways to improve that MIL-DIL relationship:

1. Choose your battles – decide what's worth taking a stand over, whether it is your children's education, your career, a house purchase etc. Let most things slide. Saying yes to everything and then doing what you want is an option but it might get you into bigger trouble in the long run. Better to do the grown-up thing and learn how to stand up for yourself without causing offence.

2. Don't let things fester – don't let grievances build up. Don't demonise MIL. Be charitable. You have a choice – you can let go of grudges. If you think she can handle it (perhaps ask your husband's advice first), then have it out with her.

3. Don't take it all so seriously – avoid knee-jerk reactions – change habitual responses. Break the pattern. Don't interpret everything as a dig, or an insinuation of your inadequacy. Depersonalise the comments and accept you might sometimes be a little paranoid, or over-sensitive.

4. Focus on her good points – make a list if you must! No-one is wholly irredeemable; draw out those good qualities, rather than block them. Allow her to be the best MIL she can be.

5. Cure with kindness – don't prickle. Don't harden. Don't put up fences. Let things go. Be gentle. Be selfless and try to see things from her perspective. Make an effort to do something she will like; bake a cake or buy a ticket to the ballet. Putting yourself out for her redresses the balance and may make you feel more in charge.

6. Communicate – communicate, communicate; emails, texts, postcards, Facebook, whatever works best for you both but keep those channels open. Photographs are essential. And make the effort to visit her – the mountain shouldn't always have to come to Mohammed.

7. Set your boundaries – recognise the importance of establishing them, as early as possible in your relationship; don't be either a 'pushover' or an 'ice queen'. Find the middle ground. The key here is to be factual and firm and to know your own mind. How else is she supposed to know what you want from her?

8. Don't expect so much of hubby – don't play the victim or hold out to be rescued. Hiding behind your husband is a bad idea. Don't get him to do your dirty work; no-one will respect you. Toughen up, grow-up and face up.

9. Form a strategic alliance – you don't have to be friends, but you do have to be able work together, in a climate of mutual respect. Remember, at best, MIL is a powerful ally and a potential blessing and support. Recognize that, essentially, you both want the same thing.

10. Don't expect perfection – relationships fluctuate; there will be ups and downs, but you'll do just fine if you are both prepared to forgive and forget. Take the long view. Commit to it and have no regrets.

11. Harness the beast – if there are things she enjoys doing (cooking, sewing, gardening) then ask nicely for her help and be grateful for what she does for you. Seek her opinions and respect her expertise without handing over the reins completely.

12. Call in reinforcements – join forces with a sister-in-law or invite a great aunt to dilute MIL and reduce her impact.

14. If in doubt, get out! Go for a walk or a run, escape into a book, breathe deeply and get things back in perspective.

15. Break the mould, beat the system. Everything is working against you? The reality is that you are doomed to fail. Don't buckle. Keep on nurturing it, tending the relationship and you will succeed. Goodwill is everything. Pretend and you are halfway there. Be effusive in your thanks, gracious and polite at all times.

Love and forgiveness do not dwell in the same place as justice and punishment – you have to choose!

Call it a 15-point plan. And now we're being so positive, let's look at some best-case scenarios…

Best of MILs

Some MILs seem to be able to get it right.

Or, perhaps they just have more tolerant, kinder, appreciative DILs. I must admit – and this may be stir the pot a bit – that the DILs who spoke highly of their MILs seemed to be sincere, kind and generous girls.

Amongst the gripes and grievances there have been some shining examples of mother-in-lawing – from supportive, non-judgmental, sensitive, selfless women who would do anything to help their extended family.

Where DILs were found to be singing MIL's praises, I tried to pinpoint exactly what it was that these mothers-in-law are doing to so endear themselves?

Here are some of the things that DILs were saying:

66 My MIL is a realist – she doesn't expect anything at all, really. She's delighted when she does hear from us but she doesn't expect us to go round all the time, so long as she gets the odd phone call. One of the first times I met her she said 'I'm just so happy that he is happy'."

"She will have only been in the house five minutes and the kids will be all over her; I'll come in to find her sitting on the loo with her hair in a million pony tails and covered in makeup. She has a wonderful imagination and really puts herself out for the kids. They make such a mess of her house – there will be Lego and paint everywhere - but she doesn't mind if they are having fun."

"If your MIL approves of the match and takes a shine to you, it's like a blessing comes over you."

"My MIL had such a bad mother-in-law herself that she was determined not to go the same way. She is absolutely amazing. I couldn't survive without her. I think her own MIL was a battle-axe and she made a deliberate decision to be very different. She wanted to put right all those wrongs. She is always sensitive to my feelings, without being annoying about it."

"She's never been a busybody. She'll say 'if you need me to come over then I will but if not, don't worry'.

"She would do anything for her grandchildren, no matter what else she has on. If I were to say 'do you think you could move in tomorrow and look after Lottie full-time?', she would."

"I think my in-laws were so pleased that he had eventually found someone, as he was nearly 36 and had always gone home with his mates and gone out drinking. I could have been anyone and they would have loved me. I didn't feel I was under any kind of pressure or that they had any expectations. They were just relieved I was a girl."

"My MIL isn't at all judgmental – neither her nor her husband drinks but they didn't seem to mind at all that I had to leave the Sunday lunch table to be sick, I was so hungover! They are all just very decent people. Even though I don't always agree with her – she is very outspoken – I do always respect her."

"I can't do any wrong in MIL's eyes – I'm a second wife – the first one was god awful! I go there and get worshipped, it's lovely."

"I married into the most perfect family I had ever met. My own was completely fragmented but at my in-laws' house

I felt that I had come home. My MIL always sided with me. I think she saw how hard I worked and was fearful for me. Whenever I was coming she'd make the things I liked best, like treacle pudding and custard. She moved out of her own bed so we could get a good night's sleep.
I think she thought my husband was a pain in the neck and was very grateful to me for taking him on. She was amazed he had managed to get himself a girl like me! She used to lean back in her chair and spit out the word "men!" We both agreed they were all awful.
I do think she did love me, she was always so welcoming – she was completely wonderful to me, really. When I had babies, she was disabled by then but she would sit and rock the pram for me. She was so kind and so nice – even to my own mother. There was no edge, no side to her. She was as level-headed and clear thinking as it is possible to be."

"My MIL has been like a mother and mother-in-law to me for fifteen years. I couldn't survive without her."

"I haven't got a bad word to say about my MIL. She is wonderful to me. A few weeks ago I was feeling really poorly and told her I was craving a hot blackcurrant juice. I'd even tried to make something with squeezy lemon and hot water but it was awful. I went off to pick up the kids and when I came back I found a little bottle on the doorstep with a note from MIL. She'd been up the garden, picked some blackberries and turned it into cordial for me."

"My MIL adores me. She knows what gits men are and she feels sorry for me. She'll say things like 'no, I've donated him to you and I won't have him back'."

"My MIL never self-pities. She might be dying of pneumonia on her last legs in bed but would pinch her cheeks to get some colour in them and tell the doctor: 'it's just a summer cough doctor. Don't you love this time of year when the rambling rose is out?'"

"MIL will joke about me being in her kitchen. She is very worried about food and whether everyone is being fed properly. Once she was ill and I had to cook a meal. She said 'what are you doing with my marrows there?' She doesn't like me moving things around and told my husband 'I think I'm going to throttle your wife there' but she says it in a really sweet way, so I never take offence. **"**

What do we want from you?

I have assimilated all the messages coming from the DIL community and attempted to compile a few pointers, to stop MILs from rubbing us up the wrong way. Here's a top 10 wish list, from DIL to MIL:

1. Please come in, sit down, and enjoy a cup of tea and a catch up on family gossip. Do offer to make the tea if we are struggling with baby teatime but don't complain if we have no clean cups.

2. Do play with the children, read them a story, pull out a puzzle – give us a breathing space and let us enjoy watching you get to know them better.

3. Resist the urge to comment on your grandson's poor reading skills or tight-fitting pyjamas. Live and let live and just enjoy hanging out with us all.

4. Do offer to do some ironing or push the hoover round. We'd be mad to say no.

5. Do offer to buy a bit of shopping but please ask first. We might have shopped and planned for dinner already. Don't pick over the contents of our fridge and wrinkle your nose at our shopping choices. Remember this is just one day in 365 in the life of our family.

6. Do collect the children from school. They will love to see you and it saves us a job.

7. Don't hand over a homemade cake, only to comment: 'well, I know the boys like a bit of cake, it's really for them – I know you're watching your weight'.

8. Do bring us a casserole or offer to cook dinner but make sure this is communicated in advance. Don't swoop into the kitchen and squeeze us out without there being a voluntary transfer of power. You could say: 'have you got plans for dinner?', or 'I thought we could have spaghetti, I'll make it if you like?' rather than just assume we've nothing planned, even if we very obviously haven't.

9. Do try to remember what it was like being a young mum with small children, constantly doubting yourself, often guilty that you are falling below standard and always in a bit of a muddle.

10. Do recognise that we are the daughter-in-law you have got, not necessarily the daughter-in-law you wanted. Don't blame us for being different. Blame your sons for getting you into this in the first place!

What does it all mean?

It is all very well to take the lid off the MIL-DIL relationship and have a peer inside; give it a good shake and throw it all up in the air.

But doing so can leave us with unanswered questions. We might have found out things about ourselves that make us uncomfortable. In order to progress – to find a way to rebuild our relationships, where they have broken down - we may need to reach out to professional counsellors, or behavioural therapists.

Denise Knowles is a specialist in family counselling for Relate and a regular on BBC radio and daytime television. I asked her why the relationship is so tricky? How often does it lead to family breakdown? Why do DILs find it such a difficult one to manage? Can there ever be a truly honest communication with MIL? Why does MIL feel such a pressing need to interfere? Is it really all about power?

First off, why is the relationship is such a tricky one to manage?

"It's true that relationships with in-laws do frequently crop up in counselling as a tricky area for many couples. DIL is acutely aware her MIL was the first woman her husband ever had a relationship with and that it is a very important relationship – MIL is going to want the best for her child. When DIL is in the process of putting down boundaries, if the mother-in-law's ways of being are in conflict with her own ways of being then DIL might struggle with that.

"If you think of normal, everyday relationships, you meet people all the time who do things that irritate you. The difference here is the level of emotional investment that makes us want things to be happier and better all the time but also makes us more sensitive."

So how should DIL broach difficult subjects?

"With setting boundaries, often it's all about how you word it. You don't talk directly to MIL without first talking things through with your partner. It is very important to tell him what is bothering you and why. He may be able to suggesting a way forward, or give you an explanation that might be helpful. It's very important that you and your partner are singing from the same hymn sheet."

So you're saying it is better to hide behind your partner and let him fight your corner?

"No – if you ask your partner to do that it puts him between a rock and a hard place. He is trying to please the two most important women in his life at the same time and that can be an impossible task.""

What about the everyday petty niggles and gripes – why do they matter so much?

"These things might appear quite petty at the time but if they are important to DIL it's going to be having some kind of impact on her relationship or ability to have an open and comfortable relationship with MIL.

"In the greater scheme of things, it is as well to consider how important they really are. DIL might be wise to say to herself 'you know what; perhaps I just have to accept she has a different way of doing things'.

"DIL might want to consider whether it is something that interferes with her relationship with her partner, or how often it happens – you have to almost take each irritation in isolation and look at it. Obviously, if the MIL is being downright rude or cruel then DIL might have to speak up but it might be that she realises she is just being oversensitive.""

But say MIL is coming on too strong, how do we find the right words?

"There's something about gently being factual. If she's saying she's been in his life much longer than you and she knows what's best for him, for example, then you might want to say 'yes, you're absolutely right and he is going to have a very different relationship with you than he does with me'. You do need to make sure you have the backup of your partner.'"

Aren't most men likely to keep their heads well down?

"It's quite common that DIL feels her partner isn't standing up for her but this isn't about taking sides, unless things have got really cruel and nasty. Talking about it with your partner will help to put things in perspective.'"

Does it all come down to power in the end?

"I think it all comes down to position, as opposed to power and how that position is perceived. If DIL is someone who wants to please she might well see it as a position of power. If you are happy in yourself then you would expect to have an equal relationship.

"I would say to any DIL who is bending over backwards trying to please – why aren't you being yourself? Never lose sight of who you are, after all you are the person your partner fell in love with. You need to be able to draw strength from that and be true to yourself.'"

Why do some MILs feel the need to interfere?

"There are MILs who need to be in to control all the time or who have difficulty letting go but not all MILs are like that. Some might have strong opinions about how DIL is dealing with their grandchildren but they recognise she does things differently. There's a respect there. On the whole MILs want what's best, not just for their sons but for the whole family. They want to contribute in a positive way and that can sometimes be perceived as interference.

Communication is vitally important where DIL feels it's all getting a bit much and again, the first port of call is the husband.""

Is it ever possible to have a truly open and honest relationship with MIL?

"I think it is possible, yes, but it takes an awful lot of work on both sides. It's not a one-way street. You both have to want it to work. It is possible to come to a way of working together without necessarily liking one another all that much."

For further information about family counselling visit www.relate.org.uk or to find your nearest Relate service, contact 0300 100 1234.

Meet the MILs

So, we've heard from our assorted DILs and I would hope that by now, you are beginning to see your own MIL in softer focus. I thought it might be fun, from everything I have heard, to resurrect the MILs behind the comments (grossly exaggerated, of course). Let's see if you recognize your own MIL among this little crop of beauties...

Nanny Jan

She used to work as a breast-feeding counsellor and boy, don't you know it. Her own bosoms stretch right over the border into Wales; you can usually count two full seconds before the rest of her comes into view.

"Right give him to me," she barks, without so much as a hello, hitching up her beige slacks (as she calls them) and slumping into your sofa. "How's the supply?"

***

She was a full two hours early – when she rang the bell, you had your boobs hanging out of a zip up cardy (your nipples are agony). You almost wept when you looked through the spy hole.

"No need to hide them away," she boomed, through the door, "we're all the same underneath".

"I bloody hope not", you thought, picturing the bloated form on the other side of the door.

***

"Come on then, hand him over" she puts her arms out.

"Come to nanny wanny – nanny Jan knows how to look after you best" (she insists on the peppy, zestful 'Nanny Jan', though it makes you want to vomit).

She swaddles your son to within an inch of his life and jams him so hard into her cavernous cleavage you are sure it must be unsurvivable. Granted, baby has quietened down – in fact he's not making any noise at all now, or moving for that matter... Oh God, he's definitely dead. You make a timid plea to have him back and she laughs her big, jowly cackle.

"Mummy's worried you'll forget where the milk bar is," she coos, "as if!"

"Now, come on, you little bit of rubbish, let's have a bit of a sing-song."

She jiggles the sleeping baby up and down, treating him to a flat and raspy rendition of *Molly Malone*.

"I'll bet no-one sings to you, do they, poor baby?"

Baby opens his eyes, scowling like his dignity has been insulted. He flushes scarlet and begins to yell for all he his worth at the monster who wrenched him from sleep.

"He needs feeding," nanny Jan proclaims, adding a self-effacing chuckle, "I'm afraid that's something I can't do."

She doesn't just hand him over – she *attaches* him, grabbing at your breast like she's Dyllis the Dairymaid coaxing a stubborn udder into life. You are too stunned to resist.

"Not like that!" She rams a gnarly finger into baby's mouth just as he's got going, popping him right off your boob. "Don't they show you a proper latch these days?

"I suppose you've got enough in there?" It's clearly a rhetorical question.

"I'm not sure," you hesitate. You know what you want to say, but it will be like trying to stop a bull with a red flag:

"He's always hungry. I was thinking it might be a good idea if I topped him up with some..."

"You know what they say," she wades in, before you can say the F-word*.

"There's no such thing as a poor milk supply. There's only poor mothers."

You bite your tongue and get baby back on the boob, while she's not looking, but inside you are bubbling like a bottle steamer.

"Poor little darling," she goes on, "what are they trying to do to you?" She makes a grab for him, even though he has just nodded off and it suckling, contentedly, in his sleep. Don't stick the whole thing in, for Pete's sakes!"

Startled, outraged and by now hopelessly confused, baby fights you off, drawing blood and erupting in purple rage.

"Tsk, tsk," tuts nanny Jan, "why you haven't cut his nails!"

It is all you can do to stop yourself from chucking your baby in her face.

*formula

Dodgy Gran

She used to have the kids for you, once a week, on a Wednesday. You were a bit uneasy about it even back then.

You would come home from work, there was no sign of dinner and the baby would be still sitting in his lunchtime poo.

"Oh," your mother-in-law would blink, looking up at the clock. "Gosh, can that really be the time?"

You would sweep the infant into your arms, making a pointed show of sniffing his bum, glare at grandma and whisk him out of the room.

That was back when she was only a little blurry round the edges. These days, you might leave your Boston terrier with her for the day, but not your children; not since the day you found Lottie munching on her bright pink blood pressure pills.

MIL is always dropping her tablets all over her house. She's very short-sighted so never notices if she loses a few. Your little girl was blue-lighted to A&E. Somehow – praise be – the tablets didn't absorb and she made a full recovery, which is more than can be said for your relationship with your mother-in-law.

MIL was dreadfully sorry about it all and desperately keen to make amends but you decided you just couldn't risk leaving her alone with the kids.

She means well and you don't want to hurt her feelings, but even before the tablet incident, there were warning signs. She could only ever concentrate on one thing at a time; if she was feeding one child, then the other would be playing with craft knives in the conservatory, or mixing food colouring in the loo.

There was the incident in the bath, when she got the water far too hot and they screamed the house down. Thankfully, they were only standing in it, but their feet turned lobster pink.

"It's my poor circulation", she sighed: "It felt alright to me. It must be my age."

On another occasion, she'd left fish fingers under the grill and sat with Lottie in front of CBeebies. They got lost in *Gigglebiz* and forgot all about dinner. If it hadn't been for Bertie, your terrier, barking himself hoarse at the smoke, you dread to think what might have happened.

You do go and visit her but you never stay for long. Her house is ankle-deep in dog hair, from her two Pomeranians, Ziggy and Winston. You keep a sticky roller brush in the car especially for visits, since Lottie is still crawling and always comes away looking like Chewbacca.

Ziggy is alright but Winston (grandma's favourite) has an awful temper and is horribly jealous of the children, baring his teeth and snarling like a wolf, if ever they come between him and his Pedigree Schmackos.

"That's it, you give it him," MIL will coax, inviting your three-year-old to post his little fingers into the jaws of the monster. Winston's pupils are like saucers and his eyes, glazed and prepped for attack.

"He'll be your friend for life."

You throw yourself between Lottie and the slathering wolverine, just in time.

"Oh, he doesn't mean anything by it, do you Winstie?" She'll never hear a word said against him.

You're praying for him to choke on his dentastix. You watch him like a hawk whenever you go round.

MIL still drives herself around, in a bright yellow Fiat Punto, although she probably shouldn't. You would be mad to let your children get in a car with her. Her eyesight is so bad, even with glasses she can't read the numbers on the petrol pump and she always has a story about how some 'hoodlum' cut her up on the B501. You somehow doubt her innocence.

She never indicates off a roundabout, professing that there is no need: "So long as one is confidently positioned on the road."

And when you quiz her about how she manages the dangerous crossing, over the A31, which she does every day, to get into town, she answers: "Oh, I don't worry about that, dear. I just close my eyes and go for it."

It doesn't help that she likes the odd tipple. Not so much that anyone would worry, but always at 5pm ("is it gin o'clock?" she'll giggle) and consistently enough to get a little fuzzy around the edges.

It's a tricky one though. How do you say to grandma "no, you can't babysit as I'm scared you'll pass out drunk on the sofa and burn the house down"?

The Apologist

She'll ring in the middle of teatime, when the baby's choking on lumps and your toddler his painting his own name in mashed potato on the French doors.

"Is this a bad time?" she simpers, "I'm so sorry, I didn't think. It must be children's tea time, gosh, I remember how that can be. I used to hate it when people rang me in the middle of it!"

"That's okay," you manage, catching a glob of shepherd's pie in your free hand.

You are used to this sort of thing by now. It is as though she has a second sight and knows precisely the very worst moment to dial your number. When the children were newborns she would ring just as they (and you), had finally dropped off.

It was always the same: "Is this a bad time...?"

You wonder if she didn't start like that, perhaps it wouldn't occur to you to feel annoyed.

Of course, you know that she is only anxious to please, tiptoeing around you like a gopher in a bear cave, but this anxiety is a catalyst for toxic malevolence on your part – you have to bite your tongue very hard to stop it from striking her.

Her apologies are no good; they come so thick and fast that they strike you as being entirely devoid of substance and integrity. If she knows it is a bad time then she shouldn't ring in the first place.

It is doubly irritating in that her grovelling seems to demand a response from you – reassurance, relief from blame, or perhaps merely attention – precisely when you feel least inclined to give it. "That's okay" is about the best you can do.

If you think she is bad on the phone, try having her to stay: she can't thank you enough for having her. She is so worried she may be imposing.

She arrives with her own bed linen and towels and strips the freshly made bed to remake it, so as not to be a bother. She can't be in the kitchen for five minutes without piping up "give me a job" and if you're trying to work from home, you can bet she'll pop her head round the door six times an hour to offer you a cup of tea. You realise your reactions are uncharitable – it is difficult to be gracious when you are praying for someone to be struck by lightning.

You try not to say yes to a cup of tea, it simply isn't worth it: "how do you like it?" she'll grimace, setting it in front of you. "Is that too hot? Too milky? I expect it's far too weak for you.

"Oh dear," she'll sigh, with the dying breath of the little match girl striking her last flame: "I never do get it quite right."

She tips it down the sink and offers you ovaltine instead. You shake your head and she apologises again like her life depends on it; champion penitent that she is.

It's obvious you don't have a lot to say to one another.

"I expect you're awfully busy," she attempts, arranging her features in perfect sympathy (to you, she just looks constipated). You might feel sorry for her if you didn't find her quite so annoying.

"You work *so* hard, I don't know *how* you do it."

In the evening, she follows you into the sitting room and there is an awkward silence before you both reach for the controller. Your hands touch, momentarily – she recoils like you are the Devil Incarnate (she never can quite look you in the eye).

"Oh, no, you must watch what you want, don't let me get in the way," she says and then spoils your favourite show by sighing and rubbing her hands together, muttering: "Is everything alright?"

(admittedly, your favourite show is an apocalyptic vision of institutional breakdown, rife with drug dealers and crack whores)

After too long in your house (and believe me, you'll both feel it by then), her facial muscles go into spasm from forced smiling; she will visibly twitch with the effort of it all.

Unfortunately, she walks into the room just as you are asking your husband how long she will be staying.

"I don't want to be in the way," she giggles nervously at her son. "Of course I'll leave when I'm told. Just say the word. I don't want to outstay my welcome."

"It's fine," you manage.

"The *children* love having you here."

The Manipulator

The little boy is on his knees, on Christmas morning, still in his pyjamas, surrounded by gifts. The tree lights dance upon his excited face. He picks up first one present and then another and another, reading the labels. He wrinkles his brow. Everything is not quite as it should be.

He looks up at his grandmother, wide-eyed and afraid, as though he knows what is coming.

"Granny, why are my Santa presents wrapped in the same paper as my other presents?"

MIL puts down her cup of tea. The china makes a tiny clinking sound as she places it carefully back on the saucer. She bends forward, slightly and, with the slightest upturn at the corners of her mouth, she says: "Oh, come on now. You are far too old to believe in all that nonsense."

The boys' eyes fill with tears. He is still studying the labels when you appear at the door, eager to witness the present opening, having checked on the turkey and put the puddings on to steam.

"You didn't think to disguise your handwriting?" MIL says. "The poor boy is distraught".

He scowls at you, through his tears, like you have just assassinated Santa.

You put your arm around him and tell him that Father Christmas is so busy that sometimes he forgets to wrap things, but it is too late.

"Oh well, MIL sighs, gathering up her handbag and glasses. "You know, I think I'll go back to bed." She gives the boy a little wink, which so distorts her features, she looks like the Grand High Witch after plastic surgery. Do you think perhaps Santa might have left *me* a little something?"

You used to trust this woman. In the early days she would bake cupcakes, with vanilla frosting and bring them round, with a bottle of wine, for you to share: "a girl's night in".

It took you nearly a year to realise that everything you told her would be skewed, slightly and fed back to your husband, as a slur on your character. Not so much as to be an overt attack – she is far too clever for that – but a steady drip, drip so as to constantly undermine you.

She was "worried" about your overdependence on him, emotionally. She said you ought to get out more "for your own mental health" (you had confided in her that you hadn't had any time to yourself, after having babies). She noticed that you were a little obsessive in the kitchen, could it be PND? (You told her you walk around with a cloth in your hand after the kids).

She always has a story about how she's just come back from helping Beryl/Kath/Vicky down the road, whose husbands are recovering from cancer. She also got old John back on his feet again after his depression, saved a small puppy from drowning and rescued Brian and Janet's marriage (Jenny from the White Hart let on that it was MIL's secret coffees with Brian that wobbled the couple in the first place).

One of MIL's favourite topics is her weight. She is a very neat size eight and seven-and-half stone. You are a size sixteen (top end), pushing fourteen stone and yet she will look at you, pointedly and say: "Oh, no, no Christmas pudding for me, thank you. We girls have to be careful."

She'll offer to give you her 'secret recipes' – 'if you're serious about losing weight' even though you haven't expressed anything of the sort. She told you she didn't want a heavy Christmas dinner, so you kept things simple this year. You hear her whisper to your husband as you're clearing the table "who serves a Christmas dinner without stuffing?"

You made the mistake of going shopping with her for your works do. You had sweated your way into three pairs of black trousers, none of which got past your hips. She tried on the most revealing, flimsy little dress, mewling: "I suppose I can't get away with it at my age, why don't you give it a try? We girls have to do the best with what we've got."

This year, she bought some make-up for your husband to give you as a present, saying: "Don't tell her it's because I think she needs it".

If ever you do raise an issue, over the slightest thing, she'll make a colossal drama out of it. She'll tell your husband she's learned to love and accept you in spite of your foibles and that she can only hope you will do the same. She'll make her doe eyes at him and say that all she craves is a little respect. Hasn't she deserved that after thirty years of being his mother? She'd feel ever so much better if you could just apologize "and then we can all move on".

She even once suggested that he take himself off to her time share in Fuerteventura to "get some space" from your relationship.

You have never experienced any marital difficulties, other than the friction that she engineers between you. She is like a giant octopus, curling her suckered tentacles around you both, squeezing the life out of your marriage, waiting for the final moment when she can rip it apart with her razor teeth.

The Equivocator

"Here's an equivocator, that could swear in both scales against either scale..."

(2.3.8-10) MACBETH

You will never get a straight answer from her, no matter how hard you try, no matter how many times you ask the same question and no matter what question you ask.

Remember when you moved into your new home; a damp cottage in the country with stone floors, leaking roof and open fireplaces? She stood in the hallway, murmuring in delight, as you pointed out each new feature.

"So," you studied her, hopefully, "what do you think?"

"Well, what can I say? It's just so...*interesting.*"

A moment later, in the hallway, you overhear her whisper to her husband: "Money pit, I wouldn't touch it with a barge pole."

Really, you couldn't have cared less what she thought but such chicanery does rankle when it has to do with your children. You work as a full-time dentist and your mum and MIL split the childcare between them.

Your mum will tell you outright if there's a problem with Michael; if he's been clingy at nursery drop off, or refused his dinner. MIL puts a spin on everything, applying creativity to fact with the verve of a Renaissance painter. She is brilliant at burying bad news, a master of misdirection and diversion.

"Did Michael eat all his greens?" You say, arriving home from work.

"Most of them", she beams (he's lucky if he ate a single pea – later, you find the whole lot in the brown bin).

"How about his nap? Did he have a good sleep?"

She looks at the clock, as though she's trying to work it out and then lies to your face: "...a good hour, hour-and-a-half".

You are lacking evidence here for a watertight conviction, but Michael is evil for the rest of the afternoon and falls asleep in the bath – and besides, she does have "previous".

Like the time she took him for his trial session at day care and he screamed so much he choked on his own mucus – did she tell you? Did she heck.

"He absolutely loved it, once he'd got going," said MIL, "so many little friends to play with. Much better than being stuck with boring old grandma."

You've caught Michael writing on the walls, pulling off his nappy and stamping in a poo – you ask her: "Is this normal?"

"At least he's got spirit," she'll beam, "wouldn't you rather have it that way?"

She will never admit (at least, not to your face) that he needs more discipline.

"You should see her little boy," she'll confide to her friend Jude, at bridge club. "Totally out of control. What he needs is a firm hand."

Even though MIL is ridiculously careful with you; every now and then, she'll let something slip. Like when she tells you what *good* girls her other two grandchildren are, adding: "it's just so different with girls."

Should you need her to babysit, if she has something arranged already, she'll never tell you outright. She'll say: "Just say the word, I'll be there".

Them she'll spend the whole week chewing over the fact that she'd already promised a lift to Nora from the golf club, who has dreadful arthritis and struggles to get out.

She still won't have done anything about it by Friday night when you ring and ask: "all set for tomorrow?" You can tell by the tone of her voice that she is going to let you down.

She dissolves in an effusion of apologies. If you pressed it, you know you could get her to ditch Nora from the golf club but you aren't that mean.

Your husband tortures her like a woodlouse under a magnifying glass on a hot day; directing the beam so it scorches her, just a little but not enough to do any permanent damage. It is his favourite sport. He knows just how long to hold her there, to get her hopping around:

"So, mum, when *exactly* did Michael wake up from his nap?"

Most of the time, you let it slide. You recognise that all this is borne of a desire not to hurt or offend; she knows how hard you work and she doesn't want you worrying unnecessarily about Mikey, if she can protect you from that. She wants you to relax, knowing he is well looked after.

You get it, you do, but that is not her decision to make. You are his mother. All you want is the truth. Every now and again, you are tempted to grab her by the shoulders, give her a good shake and yell: "SAY WHAT YOU MEAN!"

The Snob

You know her handwriting immediately – the elaborate loops give her away and have struck fear in the hearts of many before you. The parcel is brown-wrapped, with a second class stamp. She is the only person you know who uses your house name "Little Brympton", in place of the number, even though you live in a two-bedroom semi in Dorking.

Inside are copies of *Debrett's Etiquette and Modern Manners*, littered with yellow post-it notes and *Debrett's People of Today* with a single pink note on the entry for her husband: The Rt Hon Quentin de Montfort Ashwell-Smythe, MP. He was a former Minister for Immigration in the 1980s, which you think is odd, given his habit of referring to "the fuzzy-wuzzys across the Thames".

You're pretty sure he was the MP in trouble for funding his eel smokery with public money but you will Google him later.

They spend most of their time on their Cairngorms estate these days but you have met a few times, most recently at the London flat, in Chelsea, to celebrate the engagement. You drank too much champagne and picked up her handbag by mistake on the way to the loo. Things were a bit awkward after that and you haven't seen them since. You are getting married a week on Friday, at a lovely Georgian house just outside Milton Keynes, where you grew up.

The books come with a short note, on heavy ivory card embossed with the de Montfort Ashwell-Smythe crest: "Attention to detail is everything. Best, Candida."

This is new (Quentin calls her Candy). Candida! You thought that was a yeast infection? You decide your husband got off lightly with Xander. Perhaps your babies could be called Gonorrhea and Chlamydia, in the family tradition.

You turn to the other book – braving the first post-it note, stuck in the preface, where MIL has highlighted: "Good manners are one of the most visible and telling manifestations of civilisation".

Without them, it seems to suggest, we are doomed to social disintegration and "loutish behaviour". MIL has underlined this three times.

What on earth possessed you to tell her about getting caught on CCTV climbing in the fountain at Bluewater, or taking a wrong turn after a night out and peeing in the wardrobe? You did notice that she wasn't laughing at the time, but then Quentin was guffawing like a drain in a Tewkesbury and staring at your tits. What with that and the Moet, you dropped your guard.

The second note is tucked into "PUBLIC ANNOUNCEMENTS"

…it is usual to announce the engagement formally in the Forthcoming Marriages columns of a national broadsheet newspaper. **The bride-to-be's family normally pays for this…"**

You posted on Facebook – you don't know anyone who reads the Times. Your dad's mates read *Nuts* and *TopGear* and your mum is strictly Mail Online.

You read on and see that you were also expected to appear in *Country Life* snuggling Hungarian Vizslas into your cleavage and sucking on a cake-pop.

There is even a section on births – surely a time to put aside manners, if there ever was one? You can just imagine commoner Kate expelling baby George with an etiquette expert on hand: "That's it, bum in, shoulders back, and SQUEEZE!"

It's the advice on breast-feeding that really winds you up: "It is bad manners to expel liquid from any orifice in public." Your mate Lisa did exactly that, all over the bar at Wetherspoons in MK on Friday night after three flaming Sambucas.

You can't go on.

Dear, oh, dear. If you didn't know it before you do know - Candida is never going to accept you. You are greens to her vegetables, the serviette to her napkin. You even say dinner for midday meal, for goodness sakes. She's terrified you people will invite her into your lounge and invite her to take a seat on the couch.

You knew it was bad when you heard her discussing the wedding with your fiancé over the phone. You listened in from the upstairs extension, trying not to breathe.

They were discussing the dress code. "Black tie!" you heard her exclaim. "Oh, how common!"

Your husband-to-be, to his credit, backs you up, even though his old Eton chums call him Xander the Panda in his dinner jacket.

But she is on a roll now and barely hears him: "And getting married in someone else's home – what an extraordinary fashion! It isn't as though we don't have a perfectly good seat of our own. I suppose it's a question of the train fare?

"You'll understand if we leave before the disc jockey comes on? Why she wouldn't agree to a nice ceilidh. And why does it have to be on a Friday? How inconvenient. I expect it's cheaper.

"You know we did *offer* to pay."

The Stalwart

You'll find her in the farmyard, skirt tucked into the top of her tights, whooshing through muddy puddles with a Silver Cross pram full of hooting children, three collies and four more sprogs in pyjamas and wellies trotting alongside.

She loves her little cottage but keeps a part time job at the Palace, whipping the ladies in waiting into shape; you've even heard family whispers of a shady past in intelligence – somewhere out in the Far East, but she'll pat her own nose if you ask.

She explodes into a room with a "yoohoo!" driving a chieftain tank through any conversation that might already be underway. The only person who can match her in volume is her sister; they are both partly deaf. People often think she's drunk at parties when she hasn't touched a drop.

At weekends, she's usually outside Sainsbury's shaking an Army Benevolent Fund tin, talking to anyone and everyone about anything and everything.

She applied to be a maritime volunteer at the Paralympics and managed to get herself on a boat counting sail numbers. She thought she looked ever so snazzy in her volunteer uniform and peaked cap. It wasn't so many years ago that she would fly round the world with her tiller in hand, following her own boat to international sailing events – she still knows a people "on the circuit", though she will never drop names.

Last summer she rented a huge house on the Isle of Wight for all seven grandchildren and families. You had only just arrived and were still carrying bags into the house when she grabbed a bunch of little hands and shouted "one, two, three… and …jump!" launching herself, fully clothed, into the pool. It was rumbling with thunder and pouring down with rain and some of the children cried, thinking they might be struck by lightning.

"Oh nonsense," granny tickled them until they squealed with laughter: "you're far more likely to be eaten by a whale!"

They all had a fabulous time; she had towelled them all down and was serving them hot chocolate with marshmallows by the time you had finished unpacking.

Nothing fazes her; you were on a dog walk with her just this weekend. She'd left her jam kettle with 14llbs of blackcurrants on the hob. Your dog got lost in the forest and you arrived home to find the whole lot exploded all over the kitchen.

"Now look what you've made me do," she teased. "Oh well, never mind. Plenty more in the garden".

She grabs a cloth and wipes the whole lot up, without saying another word about it.

Her cottage is ordered chaos and she's brilliant at turning whites grey.

She'll take the children to school for you at the drop of a hat; the fact that she is never, ever late is something of a family joke. Your children now clamour to be delivered "granny early"; they much prefer it to being screamed at in the driveway to get in the car.

She had a dreadful, battle-axe of a MIL herself and is determined not to make the same mistakes with you. When your husband asked you to marry him, she deliberately removed her own ring in case your diamond might be smaller, to avoid comparisons.

Your other sister-in-law - a newer addition to the family - doesn't quite know how to take her yet and sometimes feels overwhelmed, but you would have MIL living next door if you could. She is unlike anyone you have ever met. She's utterly barking but wonderful – phenomenal, even - and she never, ever complains.

There's just something about her that reminds you of a dodo, although you can't quite put your finger on it. Is it the headscarf, her portliness or the twinkling eye?

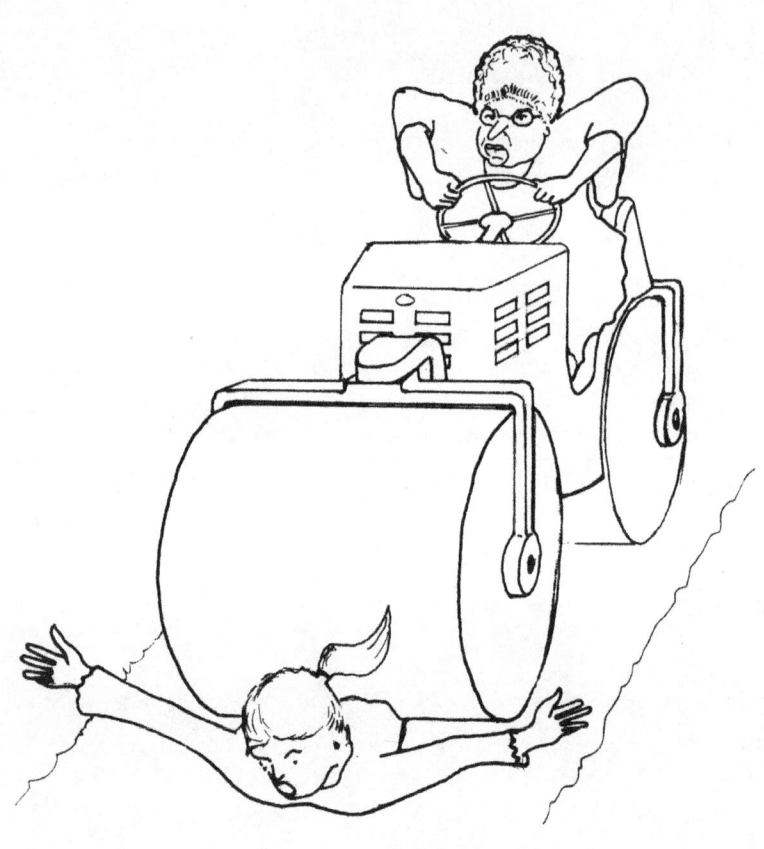

The Steamroller

"You have to let a house breeeeathe!" She marches through the house like she's flushing out smokers at break time.

"Those poor boys, there's no *air* in here. It's a wonder they don't die in their sleep."

She's still clutching her handbag when she makes it back downstairs and slumps into a chair, her voluminous chest heaving with the effort – as though she's just done you a massive favour.

It's minus four outside and has just started to hail. You will wait until she's in the loo and then whip round and shut all the windows.

She clearly expects a cup of tea, right now, never mind that you were in the middle of sewing on a Beaver badge or conveying a baked Alaska into a hot oven: "No, not like that, just a splash of milk! It's alright, I'll make do with a herbal."

You must find a biscuit, quickly, or she will ransack your cupboards and discover that you haven't been shopping since last Tuesday and that her grandchildren have been surviving on cheese strings and Actimel.

Under no circumstances must you let her see you put the washing in. She will hook out your greying bras like a factory sorter on quality control. And woe betides you if she catches you ironing. This is her forte and raison d'etre as it should be yours:

"Not on that setting - it's a wool and polyester blend... Turn the pockets out first! Centre the inseams!"

You grip the handle, hands trembling now as she rocks back in her chair. It is all you can do to keep yourself from cranking up the temperature and slamming it into her imperious, know-all face. Instead, you take it out on the steam function, losing her in a cloud of water vapour.

"That's better – we'll make a housewife of you yet," she coaxes.

You have only had slimmer soup and Ryvita since breakfast and are starving, having cleaned the house from top to toe. You were very much looking forward to the homemade meatballs you had planned for dinner – using a recipe she left on her last visit.

She lifts the lid and gives it a sniff: "We don't need a big dinner," she pronounces, wrinkling up her nose, like you found them in the potty. "I'll make us some egg on toast. I know the boys love granny's soldiers."

The children come barrelling in from school and stop in their tracks when they see granny at the table.

"You said *nice* granny was coming," says the small one, giving you daggers.

"What have you got for us?" the big one chimes in.

"Do you send them to school looking like that?" granny exclaims. You fail to see what she is getting at. They look alright to you. They even have matching socks on.

"The shoes!" she grabs a foot and yanks it in the air, knocking smallest child off his feet. He bumps his head on the oven and screams blue murder. Granny continues to waggle the foot.

"What a state! Where is your shoe polish? Granny will sort them out. I suppose you've only got that wretched liquid stuff. I'll just have to spit on it. Now give me a dry cloth."

Little one is recoiling from the threat like a chick from a cobra. In a minute, she will open the linen drawer and see that the crotched hunting scene table runner she made for you last Christmas has a huge hole in it.

You jump up and grab her duster and she gets to work on the shoes.
You have to admit they do look better.

"Wait a minute," she feels his toes. "These are far too small. He'll get
deformed feet."

Your little one shoots you an indignant glance; like you've been
deliberately abusing him. You know you don't have a chance in hell of
getting the shoes back on his feet.

Come to think of it, he has had them since reception and he's now in
year two, but you'll never admit that.

"Didn't you buy me those when I started school, mum?"

Thankfully, granny didn't hear him; she's deep in her handbag
looking for her keys.

"Come on, Sam. I'm going to buy you some new shoes. Thank
goodness I came when I did."

The Storyteller

She means well...you have to keep on reminding yourself that.

It's just that she gets under your skin. All the time. Just because she left school at sixteen doesn't give you the right to write her off. Everyone in the world has value. You tell yourself that as well, but it's no use.

You might as well start with her appearance:

With her jazzy low-cut tops, bleached blonde hair, big jewellery, scarlet toe nails, tight white jeans and bingo wings she lights up any room.

You know immediately if she's in the house, even if you're right up in the attic. You steel yourself for the onslaught, fixing your face in an expression of perfect tolerance. It's the only way.

"Yoohoo," she calls out, like nails scratching a chalkboard, "I've managed to find you that chilli sauce Tom likes – ninety-nine pence a bottle at Lidls. *Ninety-nine-Pee*. Would you believe? Just shows what they add on at the supermarket."

You know what's coming – the story of the chilli sauce and where and when and how she bought it. Chilli sauce or crème fraiche, it's the same every time. You don't just get A to B with her; you get A to Z.

You dig in for the long haul, leaning on a bannister for physical and moral support.

"Like I said to my friend Janet – we found it in Asda first, mind – not the one down by the roundabout but the one at top of town, over by the rugby club, you know where that poor boy was knocked off his cycle last year, right in the middle of his GCSEs. His poor parents. Doesn't bear to think. John's second cousin Sam's boy was in the same class as his girlfriend. Terrible roadworks up there, there are. Took us, must have been a good twenty, twenty-five minute just to get up past the Co-op – we'd have done better to have stopped off there. It's all very well saying it now though. Anyway, when we got to Asda we had such a job finding it. I couldn't remember what it were called, I just knew it were chilli and really hot, so I says to this store worker if he knows where the hot sauce is. He shows us to the right bit of the store – you know, where all them foreign foods are. It's a wonder who buys them – it's like Noah's Ark here these days…"

Oh, dear God. You've lost the will to live. Your ears are weeping blood. Your brain has taken a sabbatical.

How did this woman manage to spawn your highly intelligent primatologist, conservationist husband, currently on a field trip in Madagascar, writing about a new species of mouse lemur for *National Geographic?*

His father, who sadly died of bowel cancer before you met, must have had a brain the size of Jupiter. You stare at his photograph in the hallway, peering into the bespectacled eyes, in hope. Surely your children will take after him? It doesn't bear thinking about. Either she must have been a knock-out in her youth or he'd settled for being looked after. She does make lovely cupcakes.

Whatever you might think of MIL, the children love her. She always arrives with a bag full of gizmos (booty bargains from Lidl and Wilkinsons) and within minutes of arrival, is camped out on the kitchen table, painting by numbers, or decorating cake pops (which you are always *far* too busy to do).

They don't seem to mind her chatter; they love to hear about her Sammycat and how he goes off roaming and doesn't come back for two weeks – "two whole weeks!" – and returns much fatter, with a big smile on his face.

You suspect that she hasn't taken on board any new knowledge – or engaged in critical thinking of any kind – for a good thirty years. That puts them on the same page.

MIL has seven grandchildren in total and sees all of them at least once a week, mustering the same enthusiasm for each and every one of them. Her tiny house is a beacon to other children in her street; she has them in once or twice a week, during the school holidays, mixing her cakes and licking the spoons.

You try to remember this as she launches in to Chapter Two of the chilli saga. You tell yourself again; just because her conversation is less stimulating than benzodiazepines does not make her any less of a person. You should probably stop intellectualising and start appreciating. But, oh Lord give you strength, she's off again…

The Reluctant Grandma

She rolls her eyes when you ask her to babysit. Everything is too much trouble.

She's done her bit – she had two children and she didn't much like raising them – and she's not about to start all over again with yours. It took her five weeks to visit when her first grandchild was born; she booked a cruise in the Black Sea, departing on your due date, even though you'd told her your husband would be away on business.

She's always busier than you, even when all she's got on is a League of Friends coffee morning (she goes for the chat but never donates and couldn't possibly volunteer – she does have four grandchildren).

She'll pop over for a cup of tea, sink into the sofa and tell you all about her gout but she'll never answer the call from the child marooned on the loo: "I've finished, I've done it!"

She'll wrinkle her nose instead and say something like: "Rather you than me".

She'll keep you sitting there all afternoon, filling you in on how Aunty Suzie's cousin first removed has just had her piles operated on and what a disgrace it is that the council's cancelled the number 42 bus; oblivious to the fact that your three children are balling up wet loo roll and chucking it at the ceiling and painting their eyelids with nail varnish.

To the children, she is about as exciting as the Queen Anne chair in the living room that can't be climbed on. She has no interest in *Minecraft*, or *Surgeon Simulator*; she says of computers "we got along very well without them", yet she is quite happy for the children to be plugged in for hours on end, whilst she bends their mother's ear. If they do break off – to ask for a password – she'll tut: "I suppose they don't know what a book looks like?"

She tolerates your eldest child, Cecille, but only because she will sit through an episode of *Countryfile* without complaining.

Whenever you have a special event looming – a 40th birthday, or friend's wedding – mother-in-law avoids you for a few weeks, in case you should ask her to babysit for the weekend. If you ever do ask, she'll tell you she's having a job fitting things in and that she'll let you know. She never does.

She sees nothing wrong in using you as a taxi service to take her to open gardens and plant nurseries – picking up her friends along the way. It is your responsibility and your duty to look after aging parents.

It follows that you should also replace the windows on her cottage; your poor husband has been up a ladder every Sunday afternoon for the past three weeks and all she does is moan about the cold. He has to make his own cups of tea. She has never had a job herself – aside from a bit of shorthand typing before she got married.

She has no real idea what her son does, or how hard he works but she's always boasting to her friends about how successful he is ("my son the CEO") and how he takes such good care of her (as though he has a choice).

When he was little, she used to stare at him wistfully and sigh, "I can't wait until you're twelve", as though her services might no longer be necessary after that magic threshold.

If ever she offers to help you (nothing child-related, of course) in the way of a meagre pile of ironing, or potting a few plants, then boy don't you know it! She will brandish the result as though she's single-handedly solved the energy crisis, and use it as a stick to beat you with. Repeatedly.

Although you do her very best to hide it, she sometimes has an uncanny ability to read your thoughts: "I know I'm getting in your way dear..." but she never acts on it, or offers to cut her visit short. She never misses an opportunity for emotional blackmail, either: "I suppose it will be much easier for you when I'm out of your hair."

You often feel annoyed but always manage to swallow it and smile – after all, the poor woman's husband did run off with the cricket club secretary. You are all she's got.

The Social Climber

"I do hope you'll bring the boys to the villa soon," she trills down the phone.

"The pool is 20 degrees already. We've had the chap crank it up a notch or two, especially. They'll love the sailing school – it's next to impossible to get a space of course but as luck would have it Dennis knows the Commodore from the golf course, whatever they call him here, *Il Commadoro* most probably (hoots down the receiver). They're as good as in. Just say the word.

"We will so enjoy watching them from the balcony; such a lovely view across the *Dolomiti*. Marge says they serve the most exquisite Carpaccio."

You think all this seems a bit over keen but then this is Margo. Maritime is her theme.

She cuts a striking figure on Cheltenham High Street striding out in her Viyella suede trim blazer and red silk cravat (she tells her friends it's Valentino), her brassy hair dressed with a pair of DG knock-offs. *She* needn't worry about horizontal stripes – Luigiano (her Dutch Adonis) at Fitness First, and her Thursday Pilates takes care of that. She's as wispy as a husk of brown rice in her Ardientemente G-string and matching babydoll chemise. She'll tell you she weighs less than she did on her wedding day, although that's not strictly true as she was anorexic until her mid-twenties, but she'll only tell you that after an afternoon on the gin.

She has been gripped by maritime fever ever since getting herself invited on board Prince Abdul - Aziz's super yacht – complete with a pull-out beach club – at the Monaco yacht show. She was halfway through a Malibu miniature when a deckhand caught her and asked her to leave. Thankfully, the paparazzi weren't on her tail, or it could have been the end of Dennis's bit part in Downton.

"We'll need to smarten them up a bit, of course," she witters on. "These Italian children are always so beautifully turned out. I know you go for function over form and that's quite sensible when you're in the country, but a little Moschino or Young Versace wouldn't go amiss. When in Rome…!"

Clifton is hardly "the country", you say, but you take her point. Your children are John Lewis, at the very best. You cave-in far too often in front of Angry Birds pyjamas and Batman pants, midway through the supermarket shop, for them to be dressed in anything else.

Monique hasn't heard. She is, quite literally, cracking up at her own joke, snorting like a goose on heat. You can picture her now, convulsing on the other end, her morning Espresso sloshing over onto her *pietra dura*.

Whenever she hoots like this, chasms open up in her fiendishly expensive, orchid-extracted, age-defying foundation, which, at £300 per ounce, is 'her little indulgence'. She is costing Dennis around £50 per week without going out of the house. But then he's hardly ever there, so he wouldn't know.

"How are they in restaurants these days?" She is clearly wondering how to get her grandchildren through from *aperitivo* to *digestivo* without forfeiting her prized sailing club membership.

"We've never quite got over the Fat Duck. I mean I know they said grazing menu but really! I don't think they sat still for more than a mouthful. It was like a musical buffet. When Henry aimed his aerosol vinaigrette up the waitress' skirt I thought Dennis would have a stroke.

"You should see the Italian children at the table; three years old and not a peep! It's lucky Dennis is who he is or I'm sure we'd have been blacklisted. I don't know why you won't send them to a lovely little prep school where they still teach manners. They'd look so cute in straw boaters."

You mutter something about not believing in buying privilege through education; but you might as well be reading haikus to baboons.

"That's settled then, you're coming? I'll pencil you in anyway, or we'll be overrun by Dennis's Americans. They do so love seeing him in his mess dress."

She makes short work of your protest that that the children won't yet have broken up from school.

"What's that compared to a week in the Italian Lakes? Italy – the land of love, music, beauty, fashion, history, art, culture…"

And prostitution, you think, remembering the time the gigantic tranny in thigh-high pink boots leapt out at you in a layby near Pisa, making your children cry.

"I'll get Dennis to make a donation. They must be after a new science lab or something. He might even be persuaded to open it if they ask nicely. I do so love a good ribbon-cutting. It'll be a lovely excuse to wear my Emanuel Ungaro polka dot ankle boots. Marge said they have gravitas. What do you think?

You have stopped thinking. This woman makes thinking impossible. No thought could ever survive more than five minutes with her. She wasn't really expecting an answer anyway.

"One is so wary of prole drift these days," it is background noise now. "Take Hunter wellies, for example. Now everyone's got a pair.

"I gave all mine to the Red Cross. I suppose they're wearing them in Syria now."

The last word

Writing this book has made me acutely aware of my own responsibilities as daughter-in-law. I will try to heed my own advice – and the wisdom of the DILs – and hope that my relationship with my mother-in-law will be all the better for it, as the years go by.

I would like to think that in reading this, if you are a DIL, you will decide that it isn't helpful to rage, to be mean-spirited, or hold grudges. I hope that you will take the time to analyse your feelings and discover that you are better able to distinguish real grievances from mere slights, or symptoms of paranoia.

It can feel like the big bad wolf is out to get you but, unfortunately for you, you do have to let her in - you don't get out of it that easily - but you must understand that you can take control.

Be generous, give MIL the benefit of the doubt. If you do feel your inner workings shrivelling into a calloused, evil gobbet of resentment then open a window (metaphorically) and flush out all that bad feeling.

Start again, and again and again, if you have to.

You might think that too much tortured self-analysis is unhealthy - but if you are not altogether comfortable in your dealings with your mother-in-law then the chances are, you are partly to blame. On the upside, this means you have the power to improve things, by looking first at yourself and asking where you might be going wrong.

I have two boys. One day I may be a mother-in-law twice over. I am quaking in my boots.

The MIL Cocktail

"There have to be sours!"

"What about bitters!"

"It has to be green!"

There has been much enthusiasm from DIL Club members to create the definitive mother-in-law cocktail. Unsurprisingly, bitters and sours received most support but there have also been proponents of a kinder brew, typifying a gentler, more supportive MIL.

Gin was also recommended, not least because of its reputation as 'mother's ruin' (since it obviously has us neglecting our children and selling our daughters into prostitution).

The only reference I could find to a pre-existing 'Mother-in-Law' cocktail was an obscure family recipe dating from early 20th century New Orleans, found in Ted Haigh's *Vintage Spirits and Forgotten Cocktails*.

With a full nine ounces of bourbon, it strikes me as far too boozy, bitter and old-fashioned, to appeal to the modern palate – although I love that it has to be strained into three glasses:

1 teaspoon Peychaud's bitters

1 teaspoon Angostura bitters

1 teaspoon Amer Picon

½ oz orange curaçao

½ oz simple syrup

½ oz maraschino liqueur

9 ounces bourbon

There were a few other MIL cocktails, posted on blog sites by amateur mixologists; one with cherry, Malibu and curacao seemed to miss the point altogether – it was so sweet; it screamed total suck-up.

Another once, entitled 'The borderline mother-in-law' found on The Crafter Cocktail appeared to be more personal catharsis than cocktail; its creator obviously had a great deal to get off her chest.

She writes of the vodka, violet liqueur and lime juice brew: "This is the cocktail that you cozy up to because it appears charming, only to find that it attacks you on the first sip.

"Shake it like a crying baby… and brace yourself for the sort of attack only a mother-in-law can unleash."

I love how this DIL sees the act of cocktail creation as a therapeutic exorcism of pent-up rage.

Taking all things into account; I was determined that our cocktail should be gin-based, achingly sour and require vigorous crushing, squeezing, shaking in the making (to banish those demons).

I put our requirements to Kurt Lewis mixologist for Drapers Hall in Shrewsbury, a favourite of our DIL Club attendees). I was worried that as a footloose and fancy free kind of chap, he may lack the life experience to do it justice, but my concerns were unfounded.

His Mother-in-Law surpasses all expectations. It does everything it should. It is wonderfully two-faced; sweet and sour, bitter and funny all at once, with a slight fruitiness, without seeming confused or over produced. It also contains all of my favourite ingredients (gin, cachaca, cucumber and mint). It is, admittedly, pink, rather than green but in the event, I think I prefer it, as it is, undoubtedly, a *lady cocktail*, after all.

Kurt's masterstroke is to wipe one side of the rim with bitter lemon and dip the other in pink popping candy, in recognition of both sorts of MIL. The drink has a markedly different flavour, depending on which side you go for, but both are equally delicious. It makes for a great talking point and a useful ice-breaker at the beginning of an evening out.

"Are you going for sweet or sour..?" will inevitably morph into a general discussion about respective MILs. I love the idea of impromptu DIL clubs springing up in cocktail bars across the land.

The drink can be made in large quantities, in advance and poured into ice-cold martini glasses. Finally, it can also be 'upscaled' with pink champagne, for VIP guests (MILs?) and decorated with a floating purple pansy, for real class.

Anyway, here is the recipe:

The Mother-in-Law

You can drink this one when you're at the end of your tether, stabbing at it with your muddler like a woman possessed and then downing it all in one go (sour side, of course), to silence the voices.

Or, you can enjoy sipping candy-side, with your friendly MIL, indulging her with a pink champagne topper.

Half a lemon, cut into wedges

Pinch of fresh mint

Three slices of cucumber

37.5ml Hendricks gin (a shot and a half)

12.5ml elderflower cordial

12.5ml cachaca velho (Brazilian sugarcane liquor)

30ml of purple grape juice

Pink champagne (optional)

Wipe the rim of a chilled martini glass with lemon. Dip one half of the rim in crushed, pink popping candy.

Muddle the lemon and cucumber together in a glass. Clap the mint between your hands to release the essence and muddle together with the lemon and cucumber, drawing out the bitters.

Shake together with remaining ingredients in a cocktail shaker and strain into the martini glass. Pour pink champagne carefully over the back of a spoon, so that it sits on the top, for that extra bit of class.

For more cocktail tips from Kurt, visit www.flirtinaevents.co.uk

Printed in April 2023
by Rotomail Italia S.p.A., Vignate (MI) - Italy